Freshwater Literary Journal

2021

2021 Editorial Board
Katherine Eggleston
Sarah Martin
Lisa Sterlein

Editor and Faculty Advisor: John Sheirer

Cover Photo: Sarah Martin

Freshwater Literary Journal is published annually by Asnuntuck Community College. We consider poetry and prose. The upcoming reading period will be August 15, 2021, to February 15, 2022. Acceptances and rejections will be sent on a rolling basis, no later than the end of March 2022. Poetry: Three poems maximum, up to 40 lines each. Prose (prose poetry, short stories, flash/micro fiction, creative nonfiction, personal essay, memoir): One or multiple pieces up to 1,500 words total. No previously published material. Simultaneous submissions considered with proper notification. Email submissions to Freshwater@acc.commnet.edu with a brief, third-person biographical note. No postal submissions, please.

The 2021-22 Freshwater Student Writing Contest will focus on poetry up to 40 lines. The contest will be open to full- and part-time undergraduate students enrolled during 2021 or 2022 at Connecticut's community colleges and public universities. The entry deadline is January 31, 2022. More information will be available by September 2021 at https://asnuntuck.edu/about/community-engagement/freshwater-literary-journal/

We can be reached at Freshwater@acc.commnet.edu. Please follow *Freshwater* on Facebook: FreshwaterACC; and Instagram: @FreshwaterLiteraryJournal.

1 – Information
4 – Freshwater Student Writing Contest
7 – Susan Winters Smith
10 – Sarah Martin
13 – Amanda Fahy
15 – Victoria Orifice
17 – Luiz Emanuel de Castro Moura
19 – Emily Schwartz
23 – Dee Allen
25 – Glen Armstrong
26 – Cathy Barber
28 – Kara Barsalou
29 – Paul Beckman
30 – Robert Beveridge
31 – Callie S. Blackstone
32 – Ace Boggess
34 – Gaylord Brewer
36 – Melanie Brooks
37 – Katley Demetria Brown
38 – Lorraine Caputo
39 – Peter Neil Carroll
41 – Joe Cottonwood
44 – Jamie Crepeau
47 – Shannon Cuthbert
48 – Mason Croft
50 – Susanne Davis
54 – Holly Day
55 – Macy Delasco
57 – Steve Denehan
58 – Josef Desade
59 – Timothy Dodd
60 – Michael Estabrook
62 – Nikki Friedman
63 – Dave Fromm
66 – Taylor Graham
69 – Dave Gregory
70 – John Grey
73 – Lee Grossman
76 – Pat Hale
77 – Ruth Holzer

80 – Jessica Handly
83 – Zebulon Huset
84 – James Croal Jackson
85 – Andrew Jarvis
86 – Genevieve Jaser
87 – Brandon L. Kroll
88 – John Lambremont
89 – Tom Lagasse
92 – Sarah Leslie
93 – Christopher Linforth
94 – DS Maolalai
96 – Joan McNerney
98 – Rosemary Dunn Moeller
101 – John Muro
104 – Zach Murphy
105 – Elise O'Reilly
107 – Ruth Pagano
109 – S.E. Page
112 – Wood Reede
113 – Russell Rowland
115 – Natalie Schriefer
116 – Edythe Haendel Schwartz
117 – John Sheirer
120 – Harvey Silverman
123 – Richard Smith
124 – Susan Winters Smith
125 – Matthew J. Spireng
128 – Steve Straight
130 – Eugene Stevenson
131 – Kelly Talbot
134 – John Tustin
135 – Charles R. Vermilyea Jr.
139 – Shelby Wilson
141 – Diane Woodcock
142 – Chila Woychik
144 – James K. Zimmerman
148 – Contributors

Our 29th annual contest was open to full- and part-time undergraduate students enrolled during 2020 or 2021 at Connecticut's community colleges and/or public universities. This year's contest focused on memoir essays. As we do each year, *Freshwater* hired a judge who is not affiliated with any Connecticut colleges or universities to ensure fairness. Special thanks to the Asnuntuck Community College Foundation for providing prize funding through the Nadia Kober Writing Scholarship.

Our judge this year was Melanie Brooks, author of *Writing Hard Stories: Celebrated Memoirists Who Shaped Art from Trauma* (Beacon Press, 2017).

Here is the judge's commentary on the winning essays:

First Place: "Fourth Grade" by Susan Winters Smith

A beautifully-realized and heartbreaking narrative. The writer takes us on a vivid and wrenching journey through a memorable period of her childhood when trauma and struggle framed her life at home, and the unforgiving judgment of her peers and a jaded and careless teacher defined her life at school. The immediacy of present-tense action and child's voice puts the reader in her fourth-grader shoes as she tries to navigate the uncertainty of this time and cope with so many circumstances beyond her control. We feel her longing to be understood and taken care of through her clear-eyed observations of the world around her and the carefully selected details she brings to the page. A poignant piece of writing that urges us to see the stories that reside just below the surface, if only we'd take the time to look.

Second Place: "Misplaced" by Sarah Martin

From the opening line of dialogue, the reader is grounded in time and place with the narrator as her ongoing struggle with a post-concussion brain injury comes to a crisis point on one particular night. The writer's command of language coupled with her use of imagery and metaphor allow us to feel both her physical and mental anguish in the moments that unfold.

Third Place: "To the Woman Who Hugged Me" by Amanda Fahy

This piece zooms in on a touchstone moment in the writer's life when the kindness of a stranger—brought closer through a second-person point of view—made a lasting impact. The reader is placed fully *in scene* through a lovely balance of sensory details, dialogue, action, reaction, and inner thoughts and feelings.

First Honorable Mention: "Closeted Skeletons Still Collect Dust" by Victoria Orifice

This writer skillfully takes a meta approach to speak directly to the reader about a previous writing process and its consequences. In the current writing, the author peels back layers of the past and unpacks difficult moments that show the ways in which they've changed and grown.

Second Honorable Mention: "Genesis" by Luiz Emanuel de Castro Moura

A painful portrait of the writer trying to fit into a mold fashioned by a culture and religion that allowed no room for authenticity. The author's use of brief snippets of dialogue to define the environment that stifled them is masterful.

Third Honorable Mention: "2019" by Emily Schwartz

The writer weaves threads of moments encountered in this era of gun violence that have created a lasting sense of fear and insecurity. The repetition of questions about the right to actually own these moments that the writer asks throughout lead the reader to question the ways we, too, feel the repercussions of circumstances that we may not have been directly a part of, but that hit close to home.

Fourth Grade

I see me getting out of bed, still so tired. Did I even sleep? I find clothes for school. Which dress is the cleanest—or the least dirty? I guess the one with the daisies. Matching socks. Nope. Only time for cheerios. Milk is almost sour. I add sugar. My sister and brother left without me. Baby sister is crying. I bring her to Mother who is still sick from infection. I fed baby at two, but I can't be late for school. I bring the warm bottle and two cups of coffee—three sugars for Daddy. None for Mother. She can tell if you put one grain in. Baby needs a clean diaper. I take three down from the line over the heater and bring to Mother. I run to grab some that are frozen on the line off the back porch and bring them in to thaw.

I put on my coat with the broken zipper, grab an apple and run to school. The lunch today is spaghetti, but I don't remember if we paid. Fourth grade. Mrs. Robinson. She growls at me. "Late again." She sniffs my clothes, frowns, and tells me to brush my hair. The class laughs. I have no brush. We stand for the pledge and I miss a word. Billy smirks at me.

Geography, the state Capitals. I miss Boise, Idaho, and Ann laughs. I take the list home with me again, but Daddy comes home mean like last night. Mother tells him she can't pay the bills. He is slamming his fist on the table, screaming she's spending too much on these kids. She makes him coffee. He burns his tongue and throws the cup, swearing.

Sister and I pretend to sleep in our room off the kitchen. I'm on the top bunk. Daddy comes into the room and I keep my eyes shut tight and lie still but my eyelids twitch. I hear Daddy breathing over me. Does he see my eyes twitching? Mother tells him not to wake the kids. Daddy yells at her that he will wake up his damn kids any time he wants to. My arms shake under the blanket. He laughs right near me, a big loud "Ha!" but he leaves the room.

They argue in the kitchen. Daddy yells about the cold supper and smashes his plate against the wall. Our landlord pounds up the stairs and bangs on our door. I hear him tell Mother he will throw us out if Daddy doesn't stop. Mother gets Daddy to bed. I don't hear much, but she is crying.

Friday morning comes. At recess, three boys surround me, yelling, "Your father's an alcoholic, your father's an alcoholic." My best friend, Trena, tosses me the dodge ball. We toss it back and forth, but she misses, and it bounces into the alley between the buildings, which is a forbidden area. We can't go in there.

Trena cries because she's in terrible trouble if she doesn't bring the ball in. I think we better bring the ball back, so I go in the alley to get it.

We take the ball in and Mrs. Robinson calls me to her desk. She was looking out the window and saw me in the alley. She says we should have left the ball there, and she tells me I am a bad, bad girl, and she takes me out into the hall and makes me sit in a chair outside of our room in the main hallway where all the classes go back and forth, even the high school kids when they go up and down the stairs. I am crying softly. A bell rings and kids are going by and looking at me. My face is red and hot, and I feel ashamed. A big girl is asking me why I'm crying, and I try to answer, but I don't know what to say. She laughs, and her friends laugh. I think how sad Mother will be, and if she tells Daddy, he will come to school and yell at the teacher. When I go home, I don't tell.

It's Saturday and it snowed last night. Trena wants me to go over and slide on her hill. Mother says that she and Daddy have an errand in Barre, and they will drop me off and be back in an hour. We don't have sleds, so we use big pieces of cardboard to go down the hill in the woods behind Trena's house, our legs crossed in front of us, trying to watch out for the trees and rocks, but I crash into a rock and I hear my leg bone crack. Trena doesn't believe me that it's broken. I keep telling her it is, so she helps me to her house. I sit in a chair in their kitchen, holding my right leg up across my other knee with both hands on my shinbone, holding it together. I'm afraid it will come apart. It hurts a lot, but I don't cry out loud. I never do. Trena's parents keep saying it's not broken, but I know it is. They ask if I want milk or crackers, and I shake my head. My parents are coming soon. Trena's Mom makes dinner for their twelve kids. I don't want to eat. I wait and I hurt. There is no way to call them. I don't even know where they are. In three hours, they come. Daddy isn't yelling. Mom says they are sorry. Daddy is a Boy Scout leader and knows what to do. He asks for newspaper and twine, and he braces my leg and carries me to the car. It hurts bad.

They drive me to the hospital.

The nurse puts me in a gown with no pants and puts me on a table. A doctor comes in and holds my leg up in the air while he wraps gauze around it, then puts plaster all over it. I'm scared and mad and want to cry because I know the doctor can see my privates with the leg up in the air, and I have no panties on. I look at the nurse and she asks me why I am crying, and I whisper to her that he can see my privates. She tells me I am silly because it doesn't matter because he sees a lot of bottoms. That doesn't make me feel better. I whine and she calls me a baby.

I get home, and Daddy carries me to my bed. My leg is aching and hurts when the sheet bends my toes, so Mother makes a tunnel through a box, so my toes are protected, and it stops hurting as much.

I am happy because I have time off from school, and I get to watch TV, and my Sunday School sends over a Sunshine Box with wrapping paper all over it and presents inside. There are coloring books and sticker books, games, cards, and a teddy bear. I am so happy. My class at school sends another box with fruit and candy bars, and more books and games. I wish I never had to go back to school. Friday, a classmate brings Mother a note saying that she must bring me into school on Monday.

Monday morning, Mrs. Robinson meets us outside of the classroom and scolds my mother for keeping me out so long, and for not making sure that my sister and I have clean clothes and hair. My mother is in tears and I am aching inside. I wish Mrs. Robinson would break her leg.

The long spring in school is difficult. Mrs. Robinson glares at me all the time and punishes me when I am late by making me stand in front of the class. At least I don't get taken into the cloakroom and hit with the belt like she does to Vincent. Every week she hits him with it. He never cries.

I like my schoolwork, especially Reading and Math. I work hard and I always get good grades. That makes me know that I'm not a bad girl. At the end of June, I walk home with my report card. All A's again, but Mrs. Robinson told us that she will be teaching fifth grade next year, so we will all be in her class again. I can't help crying on the way home. I hope I die before fifth grade.

I show Mother my report card, and she says to thank God that I will be done with Mrs. Robinson. I hang my head and tell her about fifth grade, but Mother tells me good news. Daddy has a new job, and we will be moving to a nice house in the country, and we will all start over. She told Daddy that if he ever takes another drink, we are divorcing him, and he promised her that he never ever would.

Misplaced

"If life was about happiness or love, I would leave with you right now, go MIA, but life's not like that, Sarah. You're too expensive."

His words were acetone against my thin, painted-on skin, each syllable penetrating my weakened muscles. As a girl who never asked for a single materialistic thing in her life, the sentence seemed foreign, as if directed toward someone standing behind me in our apartment. But it was just him and me and my concussion, which seemed to be breathing more life than I was. Since my head injury, I knew I wasn't the same, like I lost a piece of myself when I fell. My once independent lifestyle seemed to dry up and crumble like the oak leaves drifting in our lawn out front. I couldn't drive, couldn't work, and couldn't get the feeling of dread off my skin.

"Do you want to break up?" I asked, my body tense.

"I guess so," he said, his demeanor cool to the touch, unforgiving, and strong like slate.

My compressed frustrations erupted from my throat, my words coating every crevasse in the room.

"I left my whole life back in Connecticut for you! Do you know how embarrassing it is to leave behind your friends, family, your job, to be with a guy you love only for it to end after only months?"

"You need to figure out what's wrong with you. This is never going to work."

My anger seemed to quickly morph into lava, flowing up my pale, thin arms, searing my shoulders, and splashing its excruciating liquid up my neck. Breath no longer inhabited my chest as I squeezed my fists into a fast-pitched softball, waiting to release into the next object that crossed my path. I had never felt so erratic before, and I couldn't help but feel I was watching my actions unfold like a spectator in a fight between sanity and reality. My decision-making was overshadowed by the looming cloud of depression, and my anxiety attacks were the only signs of life I had left, their strikes sharp and cruel against my body. I grabbed the purple and green miniature fan I've had since '95 and catapulted it across our tiny kitchen, pans smashing onto the vinyl floor like dishes at a Greek wedding. His eyes were large; he was shocked, but not as much as me.

"I'm leaving, not that you care!"

I didn't mean it; I knew he cared at least in some capacity, but the rejection, the humiliation, and the broken pieces of my brain were all battling inside my head, causing me to attack out of self-preservation. I stormed out of our apartment building, slamming the door behind me. My flip-flops slapped against the black rubber no-slip stairs, my legs shaking with each step.

It was dark outside, even with the 10-foot-tall streetlights that lined the sidewalks, each perfectly symmetrical and spaced. Everything about our neighborhood was cookie-cutter. In a military complex, every apartment is nearly identical, kind of like the way it forces its men and women to be: crisp edges, flawless devotion to removing individuality, and personalities mirroring each other, as if the designer sailor was purchased out of a Sears catalog from the 1950s. I knew I wasn't cut out for the life of a military spouse. My free-spirited mentality was caged by the incessant orders of his Lead Petty Officer, and I knew I would never be a top priority in his life. But I loved that boy, more than I loved myself. But maybe that was my problem? In his defense, it was hard to love someone like me, a prisoner of trauma and my concussion symptoms. I couldn't go on dates if the restaurant was too loud, sending me into full-blown panic attacks. I had the characteristics of a superhero that first gained their superpowers, the overwhelming sensations and confusion though I lacked any of the goodness that comes with being a hero. I couldn't even save myself, let alone others. What I didn't know in that moment was that I wasn't going crazy. I wasn't unlovable or unworthy. I was being controlled by an undiagnosed mild traumatic brain injury, and the road to recovery would start after that night.

I walked the streets of the military complex, searching for myself, an answer, and comfort in the lawn-clipping-covered sidewalks. Tears stained my once tight sweatshirt, now falling off my rapidly thinning body.

"When did I lose so much weight?" I muttered, shaking my head, yet still admiring my new slim figure no matter how I earned it.

I walked down each dark side street, my heart palpitating with every car that passed me too slowly. I don't know whether I was afraid of what violence a stranger lurking in the darkness might inflict, or what the darkness I was consumed by would lead me to do. After an hour of walking, I found the nearest bench to mold my depleted body into. Looking at the bright stars in Saratoga, I laid on my back, wooden slats cradling my spine. To my right, I could see a family through their sliding glass doors, the glow of their television backlighting their children playing with their trucks on the kitchen floor. The parents were harmoniously fixing dinner together. I longed for that interaction, that love. When you grow up in a small town, you can't wait to get out, make a life somewhere new that you could brag about to your friends. I never thought I would miss Enfield, but I would have done anything in that moment to go home. I contemplated hitch-hiking or taking a bus, but I remembered the lack of bus fare in my sweatpants. I knew it was time to head back to the apartment. I couldn't hide out any longer.

It took two hours to get back to the apartment. Every turn was corrupted by forgetfulness. Panic engulfed any ounce of stability I had left; I was suffocating in the endless forest of mirroring homes. Loneliness crept behind me, each step pulling me deeper into its stifling grasp.

When I finally walked into the apartment, he had locked our bedroom door. I thought about jimmying the lock, but what was the use in forcing yourself into a place you don't belong? I grabbed blankets from our guest room and made a nest on our porch balcony. I pressed my torso against the red wood and climbed to the railing's highest foot hole. I closed my eyes, letting the breeze cleanse away the shadows. I contemplated my life as I knew it, who I was, or what was left of me. My identity stripped had been away before my eyes, by the Navy, by my injury, by the undiagnosed illness that locked my brain into a constant state of panic and torment. The balcony was both calming and detrimental to my own mental deterioration. There was something powerful about feeling high up when my mental state was so low, like the elevation somehow balanced out my mood, giving me clarity and strength. But the balcony also was my chance at escaping. I contemplated jumping, falling to the ground below—not in a suicidal way. I knew the height wouldn't end me, but it was a way to translate on the outside of my body, the torment I felt from within. My own self-harming thoughts only added to the guilt I felt for subjecting the people I loved to my sanity's going-away party. Images of my mother flashed into my head, her love radiating all the way from Connecticut, beckoning me home. I knew I had to get back to her somehow. I couldn't stay in that toxic, soul-crushing environment forever. He needed me to leave just as much as I needed to be free. A week later I packed up my things and my mother drove me home. I didn't talk the entire way, muzzled by the embarrassment. I knew I needed help.

After a visit to my physician's assistant, I got the label I was looking for: Post-Concussion Syndrome. The most devastating part was that there was no cure. "Treat the symptoms" became a constant catchphrase amongst experts. I spent months on bed rest, in weekly therapist appointments, and diligently relearning everything I'd lost. As for the boy, he left when I was starting to find myself again. My creativity and fun-loving mannerisms and his money-focused, goal-oriented lifestyle never meshed harmoniously. I may have lost him, but I reclaimed the love I needed: the love of myself, my town, my family, my uniqueness, my freedom.

To the Woman Who Hugged Me

The music was blasting through the DJ's speakers as I dug into my second helping of prime rib.

"I've never seen them come out with the carving station for seconds before!" my Dad said, "Get it while you can." Prime rib wasn't something my family was accustomed to. Having a household of six mouths to feed, chicken was on the dinner menu almost daily.

Sitting at a rounded, white-clothed table with my whole family dressed to the nines also wasn't something that happened very often. The Aqua Turf Club of Southington, Connecticut was a dream location for any couple to have their wedding. The club's botanical gardens paired with the wooded barn-like chapel made for an enchanted atmosphere. Our table was located on the corner of the dancefloor which gave us the perfect view of the couple's first dance.

At each place setting under the delicately folded white cloth napkins, the wedding favors hid. In the dim light, I could hardly read the small text. "Fabiano + Lilah" was on one side of the customized M&Ms, while the other read, "Forever & Always." I devoured the tiny package within seconds.

My mom had known Fabiano his whole life. Being her best friend's son she was there the day he was born, until now. My mom felt like she was watching one of her own kids say, "I do."

"Which fork am I supposed to use?" whined my younger brother after rummaging through the utensils.

You thought this was funny. Watching my mom show my brother how to use eating utensils properly made you and your husband chuckle.

"We left our kids at home tonight," you yelled over the music.

You sat directly across the table from me in a brown dress that shimmered in the lights reflecting from the chandeliers and disco ball. You probably introduced yourself, and I feel guilty now for not remembering your name. After swapping tidbits on parenting with my mom you complimented my siblings and me.

"You have such good-looking children, they're all so beautiful" you exclaimed after glancing at each of us.

My two older sisters were able to thank you for the compliment with ease, but I looked down at my hands in my lap. My heart started to beat faster. Beginning my teenage years, lacking self-confidence was a struggle for me. Even though it took my mom over an hour to curl my hair, and everyone seemed to love the ruffled knee-length blue dress I was wearing. I still did not feel pretty.

While trying to conceal the tremble in my voice I replied, thanks, in a soft, timid tone.

In that moment you averted your eyes to the next conversation, kindly brushing off my awkward reaction. When you discovered that I was thirteen, a slight sympathetic tone came to your voice: "Oh to be in junior high. What a tough age." I just shrugged my shoulders because you were right, but the last thing I wanted to do was speak about my inner difficulties and confusion, especially in front of my family.

At the end of the night while putting on our coats and saying goodbyes you hugged me tight. While walking towards the door you told me, "Girls at your age are mean. Girls at your age are bitches. Don't let them put you down or tell you you're not pretty because you are a gorgeous young girl." The only word I could manage to get out was "okay" because I was trying to hurry the conversation, especially when everyone around us could hear.

These were lines I had heard a million times before, but somehow, they always managed to slip through my fingers. I wish I had you in my life right now, at twenty-two, to tell me that I grew to be a "gorgeous young" woman, or that I am a good person. How going to school is the best thing for me, or that I am on the right path. Even though I hear these things almost daily from my boyfriend I still don't feel confident about any of them, or that I will ever be the person that everyone needs me to be. Sometimes, hearing it from a stranger, who knows nothing about you almost makes it seem more real.

I hope your children have the self-confidence that I still lack. With the support from a mom who was concerned for a random girl she sat across from at a wedding, I really don't see how they couldn't.

Closeted Skeletons Still Collect Dust

Here is a secret that no one knows:

When I was in high school we had an assignment—write about a moment that transformed us. I had a growing list of traumas and failures, only some of which I felt comfortable addressing with my therapist at the time. I went with the moment I found out about my parents' divorce, the lead-up, the emotional labor I put in as a child of only nine years to get these grown-ass adults to get their shit together.

That part isn't the secret.

The secret is how my parents reacted.

I never could have imagined the outrage. It was like I'd been arrested, expelled from school, gotten pregnant, even murdered someone. For parents who told me they'd love me no matter what, there was this sense of betrayal behind me doing something as innocent as telling my story, outlining my experiences to a teacher and mentor. Like somehow they'd get in trouble for the unexpectedly quiet conversation on the edge of their bed, for the anxieties spinning circles in my brain.

And yet, this simple high school English class essay seemed to them like I was outing their dirty laundry to the entire world. Like it was going to be published in the newspaper or they were going to end up trending on Twitter—which didn't even mean anything at that time. It took me a long time to understand that their reaction was born of deep embarrassment, of fear of retribution, an instinctive response to knowing they handled a situation poorly and hurt someone they loved in the process. And, unfortunately, their response was to unknowingly fall in line with the choreographed pattern like a marching band.

I wonder, sometimes, if my teacher had known the emotional fallout, whether he would regret assigning it in the first place.

The ensuing panic attack was not one of my finer moments, but I have the wisdom now to realize it wasn't my fault. I've realized a lot of things weren't my fault as time has passed, and the journey towards self-compassion is easier some days than others. It's been a long seven years since that essay was written and finding it again while working on college applications was a punch to the gut.

There was the burst of memories from reading my description of the wallpaper—*"rows of flowers like prison bars"*—and the fear of my parents *hurting* each other, not from any experience, but from shows like *NCIS* and *Law and Order: SVU* which made entertainment out of domestic violence. Perhaps the first time I realized how important representation is because I had no context at the time for divorce being anything but a messy, loud, and painful affair.

I don't know why I kept it to begin with, why I filed it away with all my other old essays instead of burning it to ashes in my backyard the instant I graduated. I don't know why I didn't throw it out when I pulled it out of the folder. Some sense of nostalgia or maybe just plain fear. I'm not a person who can throw something like that out without reading it again, and while I've grown and healed a lot as a person, I'm not ready to press on that scar just yet.

I don't want to revisit being that small, terrified child who felt so, so sick every time they left the house. I don't want to revisit the arguments, the fights, the panic attacks, breath coming in such wild pants I thought I'd never breathe clearly again. I don't want to remember the exhaustion which seeped deep into my bones, every nerve on fire almost every day for years on end. I don't blame my parents for that—they did the best they could with what they had. But I'll be damned if I don't admit I wish they'd done just a little bit better.

In all fairness to them, they wish they did too.

The years have passed slowly, steadily, and somehow in the blink of an eye. Wounds healed. Apologies were made and accepted. Hard conversations were had that couldn't have been had in the emotional warzone that my household had become due to mental and physical illness and a society that wouldn't accommodate them. Empathy and understanding grew as I aged, as I realized and understood the pressure they were under, and empathy for myself grew as I realized I couldn't blame myself for not thinking about them. I was just trying to survive.

We were all just trying to survive.

I don't need to read an old essay to know that.

But still, maybe I should, if only to see the evidence of how far I've come, to the work I've put in to break the unhealthy patterns etched into the grooves of my brain.

Want to hear another secret? This one hasn't been a secret for long.

I think I'll be okay after all.

Genesis

People say that running away is for cowards. On the contrary, I believe only the strongest would ever dare to run away. At seventeen years old, I was driven to run away from my family and home in Brazil.

I was six years old when I realized that males and females were different. In my family, boys would play with cars and balls; girls would play with makeup and dolls. I saw that girls would wear dresses, pants, shorts, and skirts, while boys would wear jeans and tee-shirts every day. I made the decision to tell my mother I wanted to be a girl. My mother, being a religious woman, waited for my father to get home and took me to the pastor for help. When my parents explained my situation to the pastor, he answered, "Your son is dealing with homosexuality, your family needs to fast for thirty days and pray each morning at 3 a.m." I was confused, scared, and overwhelmed. I didn't understand, I wanted to wear dresses and play with dolls.

One day, while my father was at work, my mother told me I could choose anything I wanted to wear for the day. I ran to her closet, grabbed her favorite dress and the highest heels I could find. I recall feeling so ecstatic that I could wear what I wanted and was proud to show my mother what I chose. I walked down the hallway and went to the living room to show my mother. She looked at me, smiling woefully. She let me play dress up for a short while, but eventually took my hands and said, "My son, mommy loves you very much, but this is the last time you are going to wear that, okay? We are going to pray right now; you are going to get better and everything will be fine." We went to the bedroom and she fell on her knees crying. I do not remember what she asked God, I only remember feeling guilty for making the most important person in the world cry, and I vowed to myself never again to wear a dress.

After the thirty days passed, we went back to the pastor and he claimed, "Your son's homosexuality is cured. But only seventy percent; the other thirty percent is going to be up to him." My parents dedicated their lives to never letting that thirty percent become stronger than the seventy percent. That is when everything started to change. I was told "men don't help in the kitchen," but I loved to cook. My parents expected me to play soccer, but I hated soccer. I wanted to play with dolls, but I wasn't allowed. I began cautiously not letting myself be too feminine. Anytime I felt I had done something wrong I would turn to my mother and beg for her to pray with me. My mother would ask me to repeat with her "God, forgive me for I have sinned. I am sorry for hurting you, God. I promise to be a better man, to be yours, forever. Amen."

Life continued, and I became the young man they expected me to be. I was masculine, I went to church weekly and I began dating women. I tried faking it for the time being hoping that one day, I would believe it to be true. My parents were not suffering anymore, but no one knew that now I was the one fasting for 30 days at a time and waking up every day at 3am. The pressure of living up to their expectations was eating me alive. I was not the man they believed I was.

When I turned seventeen years old, I realized I had two options. The first was that I could stay in Brazil, marry a good evangelical girl, have a family, become a pastor. and make my family happy. My second option was to leave everything behind, go someplace where no one knew me, start over, and allow myself to become the person I was supposed to be. I never wanted to hurt my family's feelings or lose them, so I waited for the opportunity to leave Brazil but only with my parent's blessings.

In July 2014, my cousin visited from Germany, and I saw my chance. I pitched the idea to my family that I would move to Germany and learn a fourth language. For four beautiful years, I lived primarily in Germany and traveled the world while growing and discovering who I am. I learned about various cultures and opened my eyes, mind, and body to this diverse world that we live in.

Now, I am a proud queer person who believes in the fluidity of gender and sexuality. I am not afraid to make mistakes and I am grateful to learn each day. I was not a coward for running away. Running away was the most impactful and beautiful thing that ever happened in my life. I started over and people met the real me. I met the real me. "And God saw that I was good."

2019

Memories are strange. They exist in fragments for you to piece together into a story. And then you hold onto them, and they become a piece of yourself. You hold onto them, you define yourself by them, and yet I always wondered if I'm entitled to them. I've lived a privileged life, a good life. It wasn't without its faults, but I've been blessed with wonderful parents, friends that came and went, a perfectly stable home, a warm meal every night, a bed to sleep in. I went to school, an opportunity I was always reminded to be thankful for. I went to school, just like any other kid, and I didn't always love it. And that was normal.

And I didn't have any fear. That was normal, too.

I grew up in Stratford, Connecticut. It was a peaceful, suburban town. It was the type of place where you could chat and laugh with your neighbors while you watched your children play on your vast green lawn. It was where teens would complain that there was nothing to do, it was the place that held little fairs with questionably safe rides and greasy food. It was a comfortable place, a little community where children grew up together. It was a little community where children went to school together.

Most of my earlier school days, especially my days at Eli Whitney Elementary, blur together in my memory. But there is that one day that exists as a separate entity. It's a fragment so clear, so easy to recall as opposed to the jumbled and twisted pieces of memory that are nearly impossible to untangle. I was in the sixth grade. It was Friday. I had a trivial argument with my father that morning. I went to school. I had a normal school day. Everything was normal.

But there was nothing normal about that day.

In the middle of the day, over the intercom, we were instructed not to go outside. I thought nothing of it, and soon after our teacher then explained to us that there was inappropriate graffiti sprayed onto the playground. It was a believably innocent explanation; we just had to stay inside while the janitor cleaned it up. It was also a mockingly innocent, bold-faced lie that a boy destroyed with a single sentence. He held his phone in his hand as he spoke, and I remember my teacher's shock and horror as it happened. I remember the panic in her voice after he announced the truth for us all to hear.

"There's been a shooting."

Before anything more could have been said, before any more information could have come to light, our teacher stopped the entire conversation in its tracks. I thought nothing of it.

At the end of that day, we were given sealed envelopes we were explicitly told not to open. They were for our parents, who picked us up as normal. They were the ones who were tasked with telling us what happened in a school not unlike ours.

My mother told me that night.

"Where?" I asked.

"Connecticut," she told me.

I couldn't believe it.

"Here?" I asked.

"Yes," she told me.

It didn't make sense. How could it make sense?

Things changed drastically after Sandy Hook.

I remember the aftermath in pieces, and I remember the building fear in its wake. Not even a year after the tragedy, another school in my town— a school with a preschool program I had attended— had graffiti that read "Death 2 thee kids" painted on its rooftop. It must've been the exact same year that my own middle school was threatened. I hadn't the slightest clue when I walked into class that morning, innocently taking upon myself the role of a sitting duck. I remember my peers joking, laughing. When it was explained to me what was happening, I couldn't jest, I couldn't find it in myself to partake in gallows humor that shouldn't have to exist. I broke down and cried in sheer terror.

That was the only time I've ever cried over the matter. I lived through other threats. I watched incoming news of more and more mass shootings. I grew desensitized.

This was reality.

In my Junior year of high school, this new reality reached its peak. A new anniversary was added, another shooting to remember. The National School Walkout took place that year, and our school was originally in support of it. There was a vigil in the gymnasium, and afterward, they would supposedly allow students to walk out of the building for several minutes before coming back in.

As shameful as it was, I didn't want to go. It was too much for me, too overwhelming.

Mercifully, they offered students the option to sit in the auditorium if they did not want to attend. So, I sat in the auditorium. I was one of many.

As it turns out, we all missed the chance to witness *pure gold*. The "walkout" aspect of the walkout, on the school's part, was nothing but a farce. No one was allowed to walk out of the building. A security guard stood at the exit to make absolutely certain that no one would pass. It's kind of funny in a backward way. Schools always tell students to take a stand, but God forbid they take a stand by walking out of the school. That's just way too much, apparently.

It's very much an act typical of those in authority. To not think, or maybe not care, to disregard and to think they know best. Memories I've buried, or perhaps memories I've failed to bury, show their face to remind this truth. I remember the fear that shook my heart, caused by thoughtless action.

Another day during my Junior year, specifically towards the very end of it, the school held a poetry fest. It took place in the library, where students were welcome to either listen to their peers' poetry or share poems of their own. Both my friend and I attended, and we were together when the word "lockdown" echoed over the school's intercom.

At first, it all came across as a major inconvenience. Of all times, this drill had to happen in the middle of our poetry fest? Figured.
There was a small room in the back of the library that functioned as a computer lab due to the chrome books that filled it. Although there were nearly twenty of us, we all huddled into that small room and locked the door. I sat by my friend's side, and everything went silent.

The fire alarm was pulled without warning. My heart dropped to my stomach. My skin went ice cold. Having heard what had happened in Parkland earlier that year…

We assumed the worst. I clung to my friend for dear life, fear overwhelming me as I held onto her. She armed herself by grabbing a chrome book as her only defense, as if throwing a two-pound piece of plastic would stop a gunman. With seconds passing like weighed-down sloths, we remained positioned like that for some time.

Then we heard: "All clear! All clear! All clear!"

But it was only a drill, and it eventually came to an end. First came the relief, then a self-accusation of over-worrying, then the questions. Why? Who thought this was okay? I couldn't believe it. I couldn't believe that the school, the town, whoever the hell was responsible would even think that was okay. It *wasn't* okay! Telling us "good job" immediately after toying with us for the sake of "safety" meant nothing! It fixed *nothing*! To test to make sure the school and its student is prepped for emergencies is one thing— an explanation we've been fed more than once. But to throw us a curveball at us, a curveball so closely tied to a recent tragedy, without any sort of prior warning? Would it have been such a challenge to inform the student body a week before suddenly throwing us in a potentially horrifying situation?

Besides, isn't it counter-intuitive if someone's first thought upon hearing "lockdown" is that it's probably just a drill?

The fear I had harbored all this time turned to resentment. And I still hold that resentment. In June 2019, I graduated from the public school system. So it's over, right? What room do I have to complain about anything?

My experiences are so small, so meaningless when compared to that of others. What room do I have to say anything? I'll just sound like I'm whining. Those thoughts always hold me back from self-expression, whether I feel I have something to say or not. But still, I'm writing this. I'm putting this out there. I cannot be the only one with fragments, memories like these that weave into a story of paranoia and frustration. I cannot be the only one who has sat in a classroom, wondering how far it was from the school's entrance in case the worst happened. I cannot be the only one whose heart is filled with dread and hate, yet still holds the hope of change. I cannot be the only one with a need to just *scream* about how ridiculous this all is! Why did we have to feel this fear? This resentment?

I cannot be alone. So, if there is any reason for this piece of writing to exist, it's to let someone, anyone, know they're not alone. You may or may not have lost someone or witnessed this horrific violence firsthand. You might have watched a family member cope, you might have not. No matter who you are or what your circumstances, if these shootings and tragedies affected you, then it's okay to say it. This world is a shitty place, and it takes its toll, but there is solidarity to be found in suffering.

Broken Contract

   –for Trevor Noah and Kimberly Jones

There's a high, steep mountain
We, the ambitious, must climb
To reach our sweetest dreams

And after numerous
Attempts at advancing
Up that same
Monolithic rock, almost touching the moon,

The White elite above
Still can't stand to see
Any brother, any sister
On the come up—

A level playing field
Is a threat to them.
Economic freedom
Is a threat to them.

The closer we get to the summit,
The farther down
We fall from
Being pushed by
The few nearest
To the top.

It's when the earthen floor
Surrounding the mountain
Fills with fallen, fractured
Bodies, dark of skin

That shows
The social contract between White
America and Black America
Being broken.

Bro Way

Redacted documents exist,
But do redacted road signs?

One sure enough does
In these smoky and pestilent times.

Splotch of Krylon© black
Spray-paint changed the name
And character of downtown
Oakland's main drag

From Broadway
To Bro Way and it shows.

When the businesses closed down
Behind thick plywood and nails,
Polychromatic murals went up,
Coating them with words and images.
Open air, free of charge
Art exhibit over two miles wide.

Aerosol can-made homages
To the non-Caucasians no longer here—Bayard Rustin, Ray Charles, John
Lewis, Sandra Bland,
Emmett Till, George Floyd, Breonna Taylor—
And heroes still
Among the living—
Angela Davis, Cornel West, Boots Riley, Stevie Wonder—

Different sceneries in different hues declare Liberation for the Af-
ricans here in the West.
The dead deserve justice.
The living, respect—

Who would've thought civil unrest,
Shattered windows, protestors battling cops,

Could bring a great surfeit
Of beautiful paint, art for blocks?

Philosophers on a Sunny Day

Sweet roses.
Roses and strawberries on the vine.
Vines on a statue

of a dog.
Strawberries on sale at Publix.

Dogs on each other.
Thus, is love.
Roses and public

acts of affection.
A treatise on affection.

Philosophers on a sunny day.

A sun on the business card
of a woman who wants

to read my palm.

A rose on the same
business card.

Yokel

It was how
I spoke, could
not help but speak, like some
holler-born, hillbilly yokel
or at least that was the role cast
by my new neighborhood's kids, a
gang of ten-year-old, bike-riding spell
checkers, riding in slow circles and harping on
my southern drawl, like your
tongue determined your heart—
or brains or spleen—doesn't
matter he or she
spoke like an oversized nose! I wear
that memory, have some
roots in hillbilly yokel
but it's a distant costume
now—one that peeks and
flirts like petticoats. I have
no awareness, no
ear, but sometimes the idea
of difference in how
I speak is alluded to
by some stranger, who will lift
a brow, ask in third person "where her
accent is from" and I'm suddenly rags
and hollers. Why can't I be above
that now instead of becoming *her*
again, all skinned elbows and dirty ankles?

Golden Shovel format: The end word of each line, read top to bottom, comprises the poem of another poet. ("Fragment #37," Sappho)

Prayer

Every night Mom oversaw bedtime. I
can still see her expectation. I remember
she'd sit on the edge of the bed for "Now
I lay me," my hands folded dutifully. I
shared the single upstairs room; my sister lay
on her side of the divider, younger me
on mine. Prayer was meant to bring down
God's attention, love, and protection to
us both, but witches filled my restless sleep
with their child-finding powers, spells, etc.

Golden Shovel format: The end word of each line, read top to bottom, comprises the poem of another poet. ("I Remember," Joe Brainard)

Unexpected

As she watched him, her dearly beloved, take his last breath, a feeling she hadn't expected rushed through her body like waves in a storm. It was envy.

Brewski and Air Horns

Beer is the only thing that can bring me down from a tequila buzz so as I turned off the highway to get onto Scenic Mountain Drive I reached behind me to open the cooler and get a nice cold brewski that I'd hold against my throbbing forehead before popping it and taking the first sip. I was on the cliff side of the mountain when I turned back feeling relief from the ice cold beer and saw the 18-wheeler careening down the mountain in the middle of the two lanes and I didn't want to drop the beer to steer 10 & 2 because I could already taste the yeasty fizz tickling my gullet and his air horn sounding more like a klaxon and I thought back to my early days in the Air Force and having that klaxon go off at 3 a.m. for KP and drops of ice cold water from the can on my forehead rolled down my face—the first onto my nose and sliding down to its tip while drip drip the next two rolled down to my right eye and forced me to blink and close it as I fishtailed a bit and shook my head and heard the sound of wood rail splitting and the steady air horn and then the quiet engulfed me and I decided I might as well open the god-damned beer.

Tumor

Cut it

It's scarred
already

burn it
it will take to your flame

its purity
will hold your every word
your every
last
fear

but its body
will burn you

Your Future Love

Picture the map: flat
on the wall of your grade
school classroom. Picture
the solid blue background, pierced
by triangle waves;
the solid masses of color
that represent continents, countries. Trace
your fingers around the compass, violet
and red borders. Find the border
outlining the country
you have learned is called Iraq. He is there,
in the future. He is there,
and he is holding a gun.
You do not know
who he is. Who is the man
who easily wears the costume, the camouflage,
that even you in the second grade understand
equates death? The blackness
of his shined boots signifies extermination.
He is the end. The end
of the map, the unexplored,
the unobtainable. You will never reach
him, your fingers will fall off the slick paper,
and you will find yourself groping for him
in the middle of the night for
the rest of your life.

Camel Crickets

follow autumn
into the house
as if to flee
a chill we've
yet to know.
Ugly little
excised tumors,
they grow
from carpet, walls,
hanging towels,
shoes. How
do they enter?
Teleporters
from the future,
bringing foreboding,
they carry
stories like disease.
We will not listen,
preferring to torch
the residence
to rid ourselves
of omens.

Can We Dream of Each Other Without Want?

Some bond exists: a passion sense in the subconscious.
When we argue about the density of nothingness
or whether to run from or fight the monster
that chases us through empty offices
or caves that smell like wet sneakers, rust,
we desire more than this: sensual or severe.

I dream you into laughter, joy; you dream me
into a house with locked doors, windows barred.
I dream you beside me in the classroom; you
dream me with tender kisses, broken legs.

We mean what to each other's dream-
selves? We share no imperative:
dream-me imploring, dream-you embracing.

Our minds are complicated liars—
we see through them while we sleep,
deny them when we speak
of buddhas standing guard on lonely roads.

Home Birding

What a pleasure to refill the birdbath with clean, cool water for the Robin's relief as heat marches unrelenting into Autumn. The Cardinal too arrives thirsty, and the Blue Jay's screech is, I believe, appreciative. The feeder does steady business despite the squirrels' tireless scheming. A fine Red-Bellied Woodpecker has been a regular lately; his distinctive chuck-chuck brings me to the window. Also of that family, we have the Downy, the occasional Flicker, rarely the unmistakable hammering in the woods of the grand Pileated at its work (and once in twenty years, not one but a pair investigating the lawn!). Nearby, in a peculiar microclimate of a few hundred yards, and nowhere else, we've seen the rakish Red-Headed.

There's hardly space to catalog the chorus of my friends, the common abundance of Nuthatch and Sparrow, Chickadee, Titmouse, and Wren. The pensive coo of the Mourning Dove. And even now, sometimes a new arrival. Who's that inquisitive little fellow on the porch, looking in? Cerulean Warbler, according to my books. Welcome! At the tree line, rustling just out of sight among fallen leaves, I hear the Rufous-Sided Towhee. I love the migratory visits of the Indigo Bunting, iridescent, and the large and handsome Rose-Breasted Grosbeak (unfortunately, not seen for years). Perhaps once each winter a flock of Cedar Waxwing amid bare branches. The Ruby-Throated Hummingbird, meanwhile, departs the first week of October, as if on cue, suddenly and without farewells. I cheer when the Goldfinch—what my folks called a "Wild Canary" when I was a boy—takes on his glowing yellow plumage, announcing summer has arrived. The irregular visitor of the Brown-Headed Cowbird, the Mockingbird who prefers the suburbs, and, just as well, the bully Starling. A dozen years ago, a pair of elusive Crimson Tanager, male and female, that appeared after Jasper died and as I buried him between the hydrangeas beneath Claudia's window, the augury of their purring song I still associate with grieving. After three days, they departed.

Speaking of dogs and birds: If we get out early, before it's too hot for her, we can walk with Lucy to the creek. Of late, we're likely to see Turkey, a rafter of attractive hens. Yesterday I counted twelve. Approaching the water, we may scare up the Great Blue Heron, that grand, flapping dinosaur of a bird, maybe Canadian Geese or a Mallard. On a good morning—and come winter we can go all the time—we'll chart the Belted Kingfisher, creature of water, earth, and sky, swooping back and forth low over the mirroring surface. The thick body, dagger-like bill, rattling call directing our attention.

I've written before of the parliaments of young Screech Owl that for many years I summoned nightly from the woods with my mangled song, but never of the Great Horned Owl I once saw in the twilight, the tip of a cedar perpendicular under its weight. Where has the Meadowlark gone? We mustn't disregard the Bluebird on the wire, the Sharp-Shinned Hawk and wide-breasted and implacable Red-Tail, the small and colorful Kestrel with its own merciless dignity. Once only, the Oriole, but the Red-Winged Blackbird always to be found displaying its gaudy epaulets among the cattails. The Killdeer of the field dragging her wing as she leads me astray from her nest. The wake of Vulture—what strange and grotesque beauty those bald heads—at their meal or circling slowly overhead in announcement of the dead.

I embrace with reverence the geekiness of it all (don't get me started on my Costa Rica résumé and notations!), adore the arcane and incantatory language: bevy of Bobwhite, murder of Crow, rafter, wake, parliament. Delicious. I could bore you all day with these wondrous intersections, this flitting wildness, the joy or pain over which I have no control as wings fill the air.

Centered

"Don't look at the camera," you instruct, when, on that day so long ago, you plant four-year-old me in a field of daisies, their yellow middles the same yellow as my hooded sweatshirt, their ivory petals, swayed by wind, a tickle on my cheeks. And I'm sorry I don't listen, Daddy.

But you are there behind the bulky Nikon, rays of late afternoon sun landing on your steady shoulders, on the strap around your neck. Your brow creases with concentration, your sure fingers twist the wide zoom lens one way and then the other, adjusting knobs and levers to suit the light and angles, envisioning something I can't see from my side of the viewfinder. Not the standard snapshot. A more artistic image, maybe. A fleeting moment of your daughter's whimsy that you want preserved on film: Little Girl Among the Flowers.

"Come on, let's go, slowpokes!" "Hurry up!" "We don't have all day!" The boys' impatient shouts cut into the moment. They summon us from beyond the field, beyond the long line of towering pines bordering its edge. They wait just ahead on the trail. Always just ahead on the trail.

Yet this time, you don't listen. Don't look away from where I sit. Don't rush the camera back into its case. Don't rush me to catch up to these older brothers. Don't invite them into the picture. Don't allow them to scramble for position. To elbow me toward my accustomed place at the edge of the frame.

You stay a little longer, lingering in this scene that for once belongs to just the two of us.

I pull my knees to my chin, feel the rich soil, a soft cushion against my bottom. I know you ask me not to look, and I'm sorry I don't listen, and squint, instead, directly into the lens. A bloom of unfamiliar confidence fills my chest. I will not tear my eyes away from you. How can I when I know that right here, for right now, I am the only thing you see?

Pandemic Social Life

I go to Zoom meetings
at least four nights a week.
I even bought a large screen TV
because the computer screen is too small
to see the dance leaders.
I mix and mingle with total strangers
in little rectangular boxes.
Sometimes I find a familiar face.
I've gotten to know people
by their voices and their living space
the pets that nearly tripped them on the living room floor.
the way that they dance and the dances they request.
The chatter goes on in the gallery
until the host mutes everyone so the dancing can begin.
"If you have any comments, please post them in the chat."
"I will spotlight myself so you can see my feet."
Sometimes the music quality is bad and the synch is off.
My husband says I'm addicted to Zoom.
Maybe I need a twelve-step program
but I won't go to one that doesn't include dancing.

Every Night

Every dusk the wind grows
    the lake greys & roughens
Palm trees sway, willows bend

Every evening lightning
    scars the blackness
Thunder tumbles through the hills

& every night the rain comes

Swept Away

The sound of a broom knocking
against the legs of kitchen chairs, what
my mother did most mornings after
my big sister went to school,
my father off to teach eighth graders
music appreciation, and I, just
starting kindergarten would rush
to the piano to bang away with two hands
some symphonic chaos I thought would
prepare me for work in later life, as it
had for my father, but was interrupted
by my mother's vacuum cleaner
drowning out my performance. I'd
run to the window to watch other men
getting their cars to go to work, as
I expected to do some day. Later
I held my mother's hand as she led
me to school, passing a neighbor girl,
Marjorie, a few weeks younger than I
and sadly ineligible for kindergarten
who begged me not to go to school
but stay and play with her, a distressed
plea I dismissed, saying, *I need to go.*
Do you want your husband to be stupid?——
so subtle, so obvious had we imbibed
our social roles, boys for the work force,
girls to handle vacuums and brooms, setting
the stage for early marriage, no-fault divorce.

I'm Fine, Can't You Tell

News came as text last night,
a childhood friend of my daughter,
offering to help get groceries,
leave them on the porch.
I wouldn't be exposed,
an amazing gesture
as you can imagine, someone
not obliged, willing to take
the risk. I was touched
at first and then it began to sink in.
This young woman sees me as old
though I'm sure I can care for myself,
walk four or five miles every day,
eat my oatmeal.
I thank her for waking me up,
that's the exact thing
this frigging virus has accomplished,
a wake-up call.
Sure I know I'm going to die
not necessarily next Tuesday
and here I am apparently on the verge,
a pinch from eternity, you too maybe,
who can tell, but it forces a person
out of the rut when someone asks
how are you doing.
You answer fine, I'm fine, of course,
I'm fine can't you tell?
and strangely they say
I'm just checking in and don't forget
to ask if you need help and
now my memory is questioned.
Yes I forget a lot of things, even
the young woman's name sometimes
but that's normal as a person gets, ahem,
older and I haven't felt so unsure
of myself, trying to figure out what
I want to do with
the rest of my life.

I was raised by birds

primarily robins
who listen to earth
whose gain
is worm's loss.

I was taught by chickadees
each given a crown
of black or brown
sometimes chattering
upside down.

I was lullabied by wood thrush
whose song a burbling brook
taught metaphor
before I knew.

I was guarded by blue jay
who never spoke of love
who broke a wing tip
attacking the hungry snake
yet brought seeds of sunflower
who pushed my butt as I grew
until at last
I flew.

I've seen a thousand clowns

pile out of a Volkswagen
but still I'm not prepared
when Amazon delivers a small brown box
and out pops a full-size woman
not the eye-candy type but the good-gardener type
wearing a tool belt packed with
puppies and flower pots.
I didn't order this, I say.
Let's get to work, she says.
On what? I say.
Exactly, she says. *You are so clueless.*
Give me some pliers, I say. *I'm good with tools.*
That's a start, she says. *Let's build a house.*
How many rooms? I say.
Kiss me quick, she says.
So I do. Not so quick.
Three point five bedrooms, she says. *For wee ones.*
While I hammer and saw, she watches.
And what will you be building? I ask.
Our relationship, she says.
I immediately invest every penny,
which isn't too many, in Amazon stock.

Twenty years pass.
It's worth a billion dollars, I say.
Give it away, she says.
But the children, I say.
Give it away, they say.
And I do.
Amazon sends an email asking
Were you satisfied with how the product was packaged?
Any damage? How did it go?
There are two checkboxes, *Yes* or *No.*

Memory of Moss

Through forest she guides me to a wall
of stones piled waist-high, lifted by black hands
in a land of white winters. Caleb a slave
escaped Virginia to the Adirondacks,
cleared 40 acres of northern jungle
axing tree, rolling rock, ton upon ton.
Caleb, her ancestor. In my whiteness
she wants me to understand.
In my infatuation, I try.

Caleb scratched out a living no child would endure.
Slavery, they said, would be easier.
Not better, but warmer and less work.
It was family legend, a bitter family joke.
Abandoned fields reverted to birch, to maple,
then finally to conifer, the natural crop.

Boreal rainforest seems untouched
if not for this soft-spoken wall.
She swears she can hear slice of axe, grunt of ox,
echoes of great-great-great grandpappy Caleb.
In these crevices she can sniff
smears of his sweat, stains of his blood.

Stones break loose, tumble among duff.
'Roots topple walls,' she says touching my hand.
Shooing a lizard she gathers bits of moss
to stack in a jar like little green toupees
and carry back to the dirt road, the SUV,
the long easy drive to the suburbs.

Just Play Basketball

If you have a friend who burns
imagination at the stake, do not
speak with wide eyes and shooting
stars in your tongue about mentally
forged monsters and magic spells.
Spare yourself from the manufactured
shame of barbed hyena cackling
and return to the flat driveway, keep
those stories and games as lighthouses
in your cerebral trenches while bouncing
a hollow rubber sphere until sunset elongates
your shadows like an unrolled
extension cord. Wait a few more weeks
to see cardboard signs and wooden
tables fill their yard, covered
by toys with barely a scratch
in their plastic or paint. Some of them
are still in their boxes.

Beach Rocks

Thrusting their dark, jagged
edges upward, an irregular
saw blade cutting noon blue into rough
crystals harvesting laughter
from parents with children
running up across shallow waves
to sharpen their first crawl
stroke beside minnows and seaweed
before one chocolate drop dares
an escape down the corner
of a lip. Today, there
are no offices.

Riley, Who Was Small

—after John Surowiecki

It was our running joke that you could
carry her in the pocket
of your coat. She was more acrobatic
than a flying squirrel, running
and flipping her way from one end of a stage
to the other, her slight body muscled
like a brilliant mare. She rocked
a purple bikini with more
confidence than a window mannequin
in New York City. She spoke
as warmly as notes played
on a flute, always listening when I talked
about my poetry and drawings, her long
blonde hair swaying in the breeze like the branches
of a birch tree. One semester
later she vanished, moved away faster
than a roadrunner, her last
name faded away long before social
media sites wrapped their tentacles
around every household and college
campus. Maybe if she was a little more like
a koala bear, sunning herself
in the same eucalyptus tree,
she and I could have eventually had
Sunday mornings together to do
nothing but clasp
our fingers together under
the folds of the same bed sheet.

Considering Circumstances

In the farmhouse on the hill,
The brothers move as dancers do,
Each motion building to new intricacies.
Arms seed fields and carry sacks,
Milk cows and wring the necks
Of sorry red chickens, come to an end.
The oldest brother dreams in maps,
Plans out skylines and intricate whorls.
His skin blushes in a ceaseless sun.
He plots a story with shadow and sin.
The youngest, acned, dreams in beauty,
Surreal slashes of sky and soil,
Painting girls and dogs and trees,
Holding apples to the light.
The middle dreams nothing at all,
His silent body drinks in dark,
Some strange flower seeping heat.
He remains a stranger always.

Our First One, a Good One

We were thirteen when we figured out how to download our first one.

We knew already that other boys in our school had a few, and it wasn't a secret how they got them. Jimmy Wright's older brother showed him how to get one first, and Jimmy showed Jared Trench who showed Miles Tanner who taught the McFarlane twins how to get one, and the twins printed out instructions and peddled them in the hallways to anyone who'd give them five dollars. Even some girls knew how to get one before we did.

Overnight the school split in two. Jerome and I came in one day and news was never mind your clothes or how you did your hair, now there was something more to care about. "They're just videos," I said. "Aren't they?" Jerome asked. They were, and weren't. The way everyone talked about them, never in a whisper, confirmed we were missing out on something essential. Once the knowledge of how to get one—and the want, too, a creeping and new want, which confused us when we discovered we'd been mutated by it as well—was there, having one, or telling everyone you'd get one, was inescapable. We agreed: we had to have our own.

Eric Hirsch gave us the instructions during math class. He wouldn't relinquish his printout but he tore a piece of paper from his textbook, pulled a pencil from behind his ear, scrawled out the steps in short, cramped lines, then folded the paper in half and passed it to us under the table. When Jerome and I opened it at my locker, we felt the grease stains from Eric's hair gel between our fingers.

We planned to meet at my house after school. It was Tuesday so my younger sister, Cassie, who normally spent afternoons at our grandmother's, was home and I had to watch her. I put on her favorite Disney movie in the living room. It was a good one and I almost started watching it too, but Jerome showed up and we went to look for a computer.

We used the one in the basement, the one that took a few minutes to boot up and no one used anymore. Following the instructions, Jerome found the online forum Eric used to get his, checked the specs for the file converter program the forum recommended, and installed that first. Then we entered the command prompt, a mechanical string of characters, eerie as they were nondescript: dir /ab. The forum spat out a list of files longer than a Chinese restaurant menu, reams of data loading on the screen in flashing blocks of fifty. There were hundreds of them. We probed the directory for one with a good title. Some of them made us giggle, others made us howl. We read them aloud and grabbed each other's arms, howling. Then we read one that shut us up.

"That's gotta be a good one," I said.

Jerome clicked. The program automatically pulled the file from the website and began downloading. I was stunned how easy it was. No wonder everyone had one now. A small window appeared and told us how long it would take. Against the dark color scheme of the forum, the download window glowed brighter than anything else on screen. I noticed my mouth was dry.

Jerome stood guard while I checked on Cassie. She was hungry, so I put a frozen pizza in the oven—Mom hadn't taught me how to cook anything else yet. Jerome got bored and came upstairs, and I showed him how to make swamp juice. Take all the fizzy drinks and juices in the fridge and mix them together, I told him. Coke, Sprite, orange crush, apple juice, cranberry juice, grenadine syrup, whatever you have. I've been drinking this since I was eight, it's good. Jerome took a sip. He thought so too.

We took turns tip-toeing down to the basement to check on it. The download bar crept slowly, percent by percent, towards 100. It took so long that we had time to finish the pizza and swamp juice and walk Cassie to my grandmother's. Shouldn't have her around, Jerome warned.

We stopped at the corner store to buy milk for the house. Mom left some extra money that day, so I bought a chocolate bar and Jerome bought his favorite bubble gum. Back then, bubble gum came with collectible stickers and Jerome nearly had the whole set. He didn't know what he'd do once he got the whole set, but he'd be able to tell everyone he got the whole set first. We weren't the type to be first at most things. While we were out, we didn't talk about it. When we got back, it had finished.

The house was empty. We locked the basement door and pulled the curtains anyway. The room plunged into darkness, lit only by the hard light of the old computer. There was one chair so Jerome sat down and I stood behind him. We made sure to use the video player that didn't keep a view log knowing, even then, it was safer to shroud our sexuality in deniability.

We checked the door again, placed ourselves in front of the monitor, and pressed play. The screen glowed brighter, brighter, until it was the only thing we could see. The first few seconds were distorted, pixelated, like a deep-fried VHS tape. Its images shook and pulsated between lurid, overexposed pinks and greens and blues, silver static like boiling mercury, and the plump flesh of bodies being filmed. My hands gripped the back of the chair. I heard Jerome's breathing drop into his belly. We lurched violently forward from one kind of thirteen to another. The video calmed down and its first grainy scene appeared.

"I hope it's a good one," Jerome said.

"Yeah, it better be a good one."

We couldn't admit to each other we didn't know what a good one was.

Why Mrs. Morrison Was too Busy to Die

Mrs. Morrison was too busy to die. That task, the most final of all, had been undertaken by too many in the small town of Asheville this year.

First, the seventeen- year old at the end of the street. He'd received a text from the girl he liked that she didn't like him. He was found in the woods, overdosed.

Next, the middle-aged farm hand found in his car a day after he'd gone missing. No one knew if he'd taken opioids before or if this was the first time. A tragedy, people whispered, because the woman he loved was due to deliver their baby within the month, and she'd taken up with another man who had a better job, health insurance, and a house for them to live in. At the farm hand's funeral the farmer told the gathering of the man's gift for working with the animals. He didn't know what he'd do without him.

Most recently, a young woman overdosed after having her hours cut at Dunkin' Donuts. While the first two overdoses affected Mrs. Morrison, the third one cracked her right open.

So, no way could Mrs. Morrison die now, even though her doctor had told her to get ready. Her tumor, found late, hadn't responded to treatment. But Mrs. Morrison rejected the doctor's timeline for her life. She couldn't die now, not now with so many grieving the three lost to the opioid crisis. In this war against hopelessness, she was a warrior, determined to fight.

With the first two overdoses she'd fought the war with homemade chicken soup, and cheese casseroles, and chocolate chip cookies.

She'd fought with her favorite passage from the New Testament, "All things work together for good for those that love God." She loved God and her town, and figured she'd see results, but none of these weapons seemed to stem the tide.

Then one night just days after the third overdose funeral, when she watched the evening news, trying to avoid the sunny photo on her mantel of a girl lost and buried, Mrs. Morrison saw an investigative report on how the opioids were getting into the country from China: through the postal system.

The next morning, Mrs. Morrison arrived at the post office door, 8 a.m. sharp. The postmaster, Tom Randall, ran the post office alone. He'd been doing so for 30 years. Mrs. Morrison waited for him to unlock the door and as soon as he did she said, "Morning, Tom. Did you see the evening news last night?"

"Can't say I did," he said.

Mrs. Morrison told him about the report. "Through the mail. Can you believe that?"

Tom shook his head. "What the hell," he said. "I'm sorry for your loss."

"Appreciate that," Mrs. Morrison said. "Here we are feeling as though Death himself has walked in, tapping people on the shoulder. We've all just been holding our breath, waiting to see who might be next. Each time it gets closer."

"You might be right," the postmaster said, shuffling through the mail in the bin beside the counter.

"Well, can't you detect it, somehow?" Mrs. Morrison leaned across the counter, peering into the bin.

"How do you want me to do that?" Tom settled his knit hat firmly on his head.

"Can't you open suspicious packages?"

Tom stopped shuffling through the bin and peered at Mrs. Morrison, head tilted to one side. "You know that's a federal offense, right? Tampering with mail?"

"Seems to me this is an international problem. There should be a different rule on the law for this," Mrs. Morrison slid it back to her side of the counter.

"Well we don't get to make the laws, Harriet. Don't you have enough going on in your own life right now?"

Mrs. Morrison wasn't surprised that he kept referring to her troubles. Asheville was a small town, after all.

"I'm fine, Tom," she said. "Don't try to change the subject. You've been doing this job. You must know if you see suspicious packages?"

"They don't come with a return address saying China," he snapped at her. "They go to drug warehouses and get repackaged."

"So you knew about this already?" she asked.

"We got a federal alert," he admitted. "But I haven't seen anything. I feel like you're blaming me, Harriet."

"Listen, Tom," Mrs. Morrison said. "I don't mean to. It's just when I go by the Forrester's Club seeing those guys drinking, trying to forget that they got no jobs and no money and when I go by the town playground and see two adults huddled together now, I worry about everything, especially the kids. I just want to see whoever's selling this stuff face to face. I want to say, "You're ripping the seam of our town right apart and we're not going to let it happen. You know?"

"I know, Harriet," Tom said. "I do." But he set the mail bin more securely behind him on the shelf as he spoke.

"Is there anyone getting more packages than usual?" she asked. "Maybe you could just tell me that?"

Tom shook his head. "Harriet, trust me. If I see something that looks suspicious I'm gonna report it to the state police. I know you mean well, but," Tom squared his shoulders and took a deep breath. "You're a religious woman. And you've had a shock. Maybe the best thing you can do is pray. Let the law enforcement take care of the other part; you're not equipped for that."

Mrs. Morrison was a firm believer. She believed in the divine, and for whatever reason, she believed God was calling her now to do more, to be the hands and eyes and heart of His Love. But maybe Tom was right that she wasn't equipped for handling drug dealers. She didn't say that specifically, but she acknowledged his point. "You might be right, there, Tom. I appreciate all you do." She slid a package of cookies across the counter before she slipped out the door.

Mrs. Morrison headed for the church across the street. She sat in a pew and prayed for a miracle. She prayed to hear God's voice telling her what to do. She couldn't hear a thing. It started to rain and she sat praying, until it stopped. Then, she went on, delivering cookies and casseroles to family members of those lost, going last to the home of the most recent victim of the opioid crisis. It had been one week since her funeral.

Mrs. Morrison sat with her daughter and two other, younger grandchildren, who cried for their sister. Mr. Morrison dried their tears and held back her own, even though she'd cared for that eldest grandchild each day before and after school, until she was old enough to be alone. She wished she'd never let go.

Later that afternoon, just about dusk, Mrs. Morrison was headed home when she saw a stranger in a black sweat suit and sneakers walking along the road, carrying a brown paper wrapped parcel. Mrs. Morrison stopped her car and rolled down her window.

"May I help you?" she asked.

The stranger took a step toward her car and looked at her with his pale eyes. She'd never seen such pale eyes, like the mottled cloudy sky behind him, constantly shifting.

"What have you got there, in that package?" she asked sharply.

The man turned away and began walking again, as if he'd considered her and decided it best not to engage with her at all.

Mrs. Morrison thought about the little pills, and the drug companies that sold them. She thought about the investigative news stories that chronicled the profit and the greed. She thought of all the meals she'd cooked, tears she'd dried, prayers she'd uttered. She thought about what Tom Randall had cautioned, that she wasn't equipped for policing criminal acts.

And she decided to give this man one last chance. She pulled her car up along side him again, window open. "I'm not going to ask again. What's in that package? Is it drugs?"

The man said nothing, but as he lifted his hood up around his ears, as if protection against her voice and her questions.

And he kept walking.

The road was deserted, the playground empty, lights out at the post office. The river ran swift with rain.

Mrs. Morrison waited just long enough, then she pressed her foot to the gas and shot forward, closing her eyes and letting her prayers loose with the thunk and thump of the man's body against the hood of her car. She closed her eyes so as not to see his face looking at her through the glass as she made straight for the river. When the car hit the water, Mrs. Morrison opened her eyes to see the man and the package washing clear out of town and above her, she saw the wavering stars of a world underwater.

Remainders

When you die, I will unfurl your skin from your body
as if you were an apple or a pheasant, carefully cut your tattoos
from your flayed skin for future preservation. When you die,
I will carefully package your organs for their various destinations,
send them off like Christmas presents to waiting hosts around the world.
When you die, I will make sure every drop of blood
finds its way into a labeled plastic sack,
I will make sure your bones are cleaned and dried
and varnished for preservation.
Everything has its place. Nothing will be wasted.

There are instructions left for my own body, too—I will not abide
horse-drawn processions, a parade of black cars
gloomy-faced children in ill-fitting church clothes
a solemn ceremony involving too many dead flowers
a noisy mechanism lowering my casket into the ground.
I would rather have bits of me scattered into the sea like popcorn for seagulls
rolled off the back of a rickety old truck for lions to fight over
propped up in a shooting range to test the damage caused by various bullet
    calibers
dragged off into the bushes by feral dogs or ambitious raccoons.

Deep

By all accounts, he was a normal guy. He was painfully quiet these days, but given what had happened, it was understandable. Every day, he went to work and came home, went grocery shopping every Saturday, visited with friends once in a while, and that was about it.

He had one quirk to him that was rather unusual but by no means punishable. He would sit at the edge of the dock on the lake behind his home every evening. When the sun would be setting gold and the breeze was pulling the leaves of the trees ever so gently, he was there. When the days were short and the rain was beating down with the wrath of an angry god, he was there. His feet were in the water, and his head was tilted downward.

At the same time of every day, he would see them. They were two small, pale faces coming up from the murky water, never coming close enough to the surface to be touched, but just far enough to be visible. Far beneath the water, they appear as though they glow. He sees one is a woman, with fine, red hair that dances around her in the water, every so often gliding across her staring face. The other, a child. A look of longing rests on his chubby face as he clings to her. They say nothing, and he says nothing, and after a few moments, they sink back down out of his view. This is the worst part. He sighs, stays a moment more, then reluctantly pulls his feet from the water and makes the lonely short walk back to his home.

"Someday," he'd say to himself. "But not yet."

Every day for seven years he would do this, the same ritual, unchanging. On days he would miss the visit, he would be unable to sleep the night, racked with guilt. He would think of the last time he spoke to them, his wife and child, years ago, over and over and over. "Be safe, a storm is supposed to be rolling in in the evening. Take life jackets." They had only just moved here. They didn't understand just yet the power a raging storm can have on a wide lake and a tiny wooden canoe. They were just so excited to live on the water and enjoy their new life. His wife smiled and jokingly rolled her eyes. "All right, all right, we'll take some."

For whatever reason, she didn't, and the storm arrived earlier than it was forecasted. Their boat was tipped and the mother and son did not make it. It was a couple of days before they were found. At least, people would whisper, they died together. This wasn't much condolence to the man who was now left behind.

His days that followed were full of solitude and replaying old, cold memories as though they were on tape. Each night he watched his own wedding through his mind's eye, the birth of his son, the way she broke her heel on their first date, and how excited she was to show him her newly dyed hair. Each morning he would remember his son across the table, his mouth full of cheerios with a spoon gripped tightly in his left hand. His life now felt like a rewind, his scrambling mind never allowing him to take another step forward without them.

His only respite was seeing their faces at the dock, and so he sat there every evening. He told himself he needed to see them as not to forget what they looked like. One year melted into the other, but he never really noticed. All that existed was the desire to see them and have them be a part of him once more.

Finally, on the first day of the eighth year of visiting the dock, he decided it had been long enough. He walked to the dock, sat at the end, and waited. His heart beat a little faster this time, though he kept his composure.

They came as they always do, silently beckoning him to come to them, their young innocent eyes telling him he is missed. With his clothes and shoes on he slipped off the end of the dock and into the freezing cold water.

At first, he felt nothing but cold as he waited patiently to sink. Then, a hand. And another. He opened his eyes, but through the murk and fog, he could barely see more than he could above. But he knew. He touched the soft, round faces of his wife and child for the first time since the day they drowned, and together they went further and further into the depths. The cold had never felt so warm and inviting. For the first time in eight years, his shoulders relaxed as the tension and guilt seeped away. Every poisonous thought of how cruel the world was slipped from his mind, being replaced by memories of love and light.

"I love you," he said, his last words. They came out as three oblong bubbles rising up to the light of the surface. The silence following echoed the only peace his mind had had in years. He slipped down into the dark depths without a single doubt or concern, just thankful to finally have a conclusion to his pain.

He was found the next day, bobbing up and down in the gentle waters like an apple. His corpse had a melancholy smile and small red lines across his hands. He looked at peace. Locals shook their heads slowly in sadness when it hit the news. "It's too bad he died alone," they would say. By all accounts, he had seemed like a normal guy. Painfully quiet, understandably, but normal nonetheless.

This lake is known locally for its freshwater jellyfish. They are small, pale creatures that come up from the murky water, never coming close enough to the surface to be touched, but just far enough to be visible. Far beneath the water, they can appear as though they glow.

A Rainy Evening in October

Unusually for you
you were quiet
didn't say a word
I said a few things
not much
told you that the house looked well
though it was strange
to see the gates closed

caught you up with family news
the local goings on
nothings and more nothings
my daughter took over then
the little girl who
on the drive over
had been worried
unsure of what to say

she told you about her new teacher
how it is so important for everyone to wash their hands
and to use sanitiser afterward
how she loves football now and how
her teeth aren't growing
quite as quickly as expected

it was a strange visit
different to those before and honestly
I'm not sure
if we will come again
I'm not sure
if you would want us to

as we were leaving
the rain was falling hard
though it was not cold
and the cemetery gate
creaked loudly behind us

Sands in the Eternal Night

She sat at the edge of the crashing ocean,
Staring into the dark abyss that held a
simple harmonic motion,
Awaiting her lover, as the last of the
daylight did fade,
Her love, a smile betrayed,
Her aura, the setting sun did set aglow,
Silhouetted against the dimming sky, and
the winds that blow,
And as the fire was extinguished by the sea,
A pale figure on the horizon was seen,
Whose whispers trailed on the salty breeze,
Making her heart flutter, as the shadows did flee,
And when the night silently fell,
They created a bed, of sand and shell,
And between smiles, and sweet nothings shared,
For a fleeting moment they were paired,
From your flowing gown, grain by grain,
the stars are put to the sky,
From your ivory pallor, the moon doth shine,
The weave of your golden hair, as strong as
my bones are brittle,
Your touch, a shared committal,
In your arms I long to be,
As our eyes see the flow of eternity,
To dream the dreams, of poets long dead,
To speak the words that have never been said,
And yet, at dawn, we regretfully depart,
Swirling memories, and decaying hearts,
Whose tears create the primordial waters
from which life came,
So we can dance again, amid souls reclaimed,
Ever shall we meet for transient kisses,
Among the sweetest of reminisces,
For your sands flow on, into the eternal night,
As your smile is all living creatures final sight,
For time, and death have never changed,
Fate hath decreed our love, pre-ordained.

City Feller

When my sideways Uncle Dale flies back in
from Charlotte, he puts a big thing of Cool

Whip all over his slice of apple pie and blows
my mind. I have a picture of me watching him

at table: my red hair flat to skull, green bean
skinny with a striped polo shirt buttoned up

to my neck and a gap between my front teeth
like the space between parked cars. Fascinated

by the sound of air when he pushes down on
the nozzle and sprays that white froth all over

his dessert. I think that's why when he comes,
he's happier to see me than the rest of the family.

Frozen River

Some physicists say (not Einstein) that time
is not like a river flowing
from the past through the present
into the future but instead a frozen river
no past or future no flowing of anything anywhere
everything that's ever happened
or is happening or will happen is there already
frozen together (this is not the easiest
concept in the world to grasp)
time doesn't move
just sits there in a big block of ice.
So theoretically I'm in our living room
back in our house on Northfield Avenue
Mom's on the sofa watching TV
Gunsmoke or Perry Mason and I'm ten running
my Matchbox cars up and down the hills and valleys
that are her arms and legs
and I haven't a care in the world.

The Bright Side

    –for Alan

Some days the depression rolls over me like a rogue wave
all feels like such a waste of time and so dangerous
but we try to keep busy
at least distracted, have projects to keep us occupied
that helps a lot
sitting around hand-wringing is not helpful.
(We have friends in town, oldsters like us
who watch the news all damn day long!
I'd be up on the roof so fast your head would spin.)
Fortunately on the bright side of this horror show
we're retired
have no children to shelter, feed and educate
no jobs to worry about losing
no classes to attend
just go once a week to the grocery store
just leave our "4 walls" once a week to go to the grocery store
7am during the time set aside for the oldsters
hunker down the rest of the time and wait it out . . .

Heartbeat

Press a cookie cutter to my chest
and carve a heart out from my flesh.
Though perfect to the naked eye,
it lacks a certain symmetry.
It falls flat—incomplete.
A heart of this flesh will never beat.

In Search Of: Longmeadow

–A Defenestration in Five Acts (a True Story)

SETTING:
ONLINE IN THE AUTUMN OF OUR DESPAIR 2020

SCENE:
FACEBOOK USER GROUP: LONGMEADOW AREA ISO

A page for people to post ISO. Also a much easier way to sell your items. No hassle of making albums just to end up not selling the item anyway. Longmeadow Area ISO is an easier way for buyers and sellers to connect. Please keep all posts appropriate. Admins will remove any person that is disrespectful, inappropriate or does not behave in an adult like manner. Rules will be modified as necessary. Thanks for joining and we hope that you find everything that you are ISO!

Absolutely NO ISO car seats, formula or breast pumps!

FIRST POST:
August 28, 2020 (from a pit of anxious boredom)

David Fromm (is feeling lonely) to LM Area ISO:

ISO dog rental. New to town, you guys have a lot of wonderful dogs here. Short dogs, tall dogs, skinny dogs, fat dogs. Where do you rent your dogs? I would like to rent a dog that looks like the dog I had as a youth—a Bichon-Weimaraner blend who answered to the name Cleve. Not sure what his given name was. Anyway, I'd like to rent a similar dog, just for a couple of hours, to watch tv with. Cleve used to love watching Magnum P. I. and the PBS Newshour. Didn't we all? Simpler times. Simpler times. Would be helpful if rental dog was named Cleve or could at least act like that was his or her name. Any leads appreciated.

Response: 62 laughter emoji, 9 likes, 2 loves, 30 comments including referrals to shelters, admonishments and several offers to lend poster dogs, children and/or spouses

SECOND POST:
September 4, 2020 (emboldened)

David Fromm (is feeling hungry) to LM Area ISO:

> ISO pizza service. New in town, you guys have a lot of great pizza. Large ones, small ones, mostly round but they can be square too. And the toppings—it's like that old joke: "If you don't like the pizza in Massachusetts, wait five minutes!" I never did get that joke but what I did get is enjoying a pizza pie with my dog Cleve while watching the PBS Newshour back in my youth. Simpler times. Anyway here's the problem. I don't drive anymore—I can, but I don't. Not unless I have to. It's too risky. I'm looking for a service that can get the pizza from the pizza factory to my house without me having to get up from this here BarcaLounger. A pizza taxi, so to say. I order it, pizza taxi guy goes, picks it up, brings it to me. Seems like a no brainer, right? Actually I'm surprised the pizza factories haven't already come up with something. Any leads appreciated.

Response: 9 laughter emoji, 42 comments, 40 of which include referrals to preferred pizza restaurants and two of which are requests to "stahhhhp."

THIRD POST:
September 11, 2020 (already addicted)

David Fromm (is feeling anxious) to LM Area ISO:

> ISO duck tape. New in town, you folks have some wonderful ducks up here. My rental dog Cleve is a light sleeper and the only thing that helps him go down is the sound of ducks quacking on the cornfield. With the winter approaching, I am concerned that all the ducks will be heading north pursuant to the terms of their treaty with the geese and it will be hard to find duck sounds. I have tried putting my hands together in front of my mouth and repeating the word "duck" but it seems to agitate Cleve. Recently I heard about duck tape, which sounds like an answer to my prayers. ISO recommendations as to where to acquire such a tape. I will also need a cornfield, I suppose. Any leads appreciated.

Response: Post not approved by admins. Third-party reviews suggest it is nonetheless funny.

FOURTH POST:
October 9, 2020 (undaunted; perhaps it was an oversight)

David Fromm (is feeling festive) to LM Area ISO:

> ISO, like, a loooooong metal antenna. My rental dog Cleve and I have been working on a "monster" of a project for Halloween and I don't want to say too much about it but to be "frank" it might just challenge all of our assumptions about life and the soul and the Hippocratic Oath. We've "assembled" all the other "parts" and just need a good thunderstorm to come along and hopefully "jolt" some "life" into our "stitched-up cadaver"—lol just kidding. Anyway, if you have a really long antenna, and some big lug nuts, let me know! What could go wrong?

Response: Post also not approved by admins. Third-party reviews are mixed.

FIFTH (AND FINAL) POST:
October 16, 2020 (well then, he huffs)

David Fromm (is feeling confused) to LM Area ISO:

> ISO a local ISO alternative to LM Area ISO. New in town, you guys have a great ISO community here. When I first arrived I used LM Area ISO to obtain my rental dog Cleve, my constant companion at least until the 23rd, and thereafter availed myself of the service to locate great pizza taxis. Subsequent posts seeking a Bon Jovi impersonator [not included above], non-traditional holiday décor [also not included above], and a long metal antenna, however, did not generate helpful responses. In fact I do not even see the posts on your page. Maybe it is my computer? I am working on a Commodore, 64 with sciatica— me, not the Commodore—I have never been in the Navy. But anyway I am a big believer in ISO pages in fact in my last town I met my ex-wife on an ISO page when I responded to her post seeking an ex-husband, and I would like to participate in this ISO community to share your knowledge. Is anybody able to see this? Hello?

Response: Post not approved by admins. Days later poster apologizes privately to admins in Messenger. Poster advised that admins do not approve of these posts and will not entertain further. Third-party reviews profess astonishment at use of real name and include one comment to the effect of "all that talent and this is what you choose to do with it?"

fin

Live Fast and Die Young

> "Climate change may make trees live fast and die young"
> —Adam Vaughn in *Environment*

If you can't stand the heat, get out of town—
go north, young ponderosa pine, young oak,

or learn to fly your seed like thistledown.
Climate change moves too fast for rooted folk.

The ancient trees are falling as we speak,
so now we plant saplings from way down south.

Can they adapt to jetlag, learn to eke
out brief life-cycles from disaster's mouth?

PG&E cut down our mountain pine
young, graceful, aspiring to stately form,

for fear the tree might fall across their line
sparking conflagration—our new-found norm.

What is a world without our breathing trees,
sweet birdsong boughs in a green leafy breeze?

Día de los Muertos

    –a paradigm

How do the dead live?
Marigolds, a framed photo.

What music is this?
Fado of longing,
mariachi of brave joy.

Ofrendas bright as
farmers market of harvest—
dead sister, grandson,
generations in memory.
Now he lights incense,
blesses, purifies the skull
of a faithful dog,
wraps it in spotless linen
to carry it with him home.

The scene is dreamlike
as if seen through human tears—
a woman closes
eyes, cradles her lips around
the tones of *La Llorona*.

Beat of native drums
and the skeleton dancers
keep its dark deep pulse—
dancing with sun-gold feathers
flying at forearm and knee.

Dancer whirls and stomps,
drops to his knees and rises—
a bird's hollow bones.

Your Echocardiogram

A flashlight illuminates clouds
on a dark river tiding underground,
at times reflecting red neon then blue,
then white on black again.
Silence. An audible *glub* at intervals.
The surface light-show cloaks
who-knows what depths. Storm-
drain suddenly exposed
in an unknown town where we've
been living all these years.
A tech draws figures on the screen
as if to bridge or bank the tide.
Dark water finds a grid—an oval
of woven wire, field-fence
to keep our sheep at pasture—
disappearing into deep-dark water
under clouds or foam, illusion
of searching for a young boy drowned
beyond the canny of a dog's nose.
At last the image soothes,
a single light post rippling like
a signal-beam from shore.
Only the doctor will say what it means.

The Power of Yellow

A Crayola sixty-four pack allowed the children to pick themes for injecting color into a cloudy day. Tallis, inspired by her father's Van Gogh print, suggested, "Let's do yellow today. All yellow."

Janiel and Susu followed Tallis's eyes to the framed poster. They looked at each other, nodded, then selected their colors: Banana Mania, Goldenrod, Canary. They drew the vase, arranged the sunflowers, and were transported to Vincent's yellow house in southern France, into the room he'd decorated for Gauguin. The three friends didn't know the story behind the scene but in tangy, scented wax they captured Vincent's hope and optimism—the same promise that flowed through viscous oils more than a century earlier.

As work progressed, their colors turned darker: Tumbleweed, Burnt Orange, Apricot. Hope diminished. Madness increased.

Janiel asked, "Shouldn't yellow flowers be brighter?"

"Maybe they were shinier outdoors, waving in the breeze, following the sun," Tallis replied.

"I have a neon twenty-four pack of crayons in my knapsack," Susu offered. "With Laser Lemon and Sunglow, we can draw sunflowers like the ones growing along highway six, every August."

Their palette brighter and sunnier, a rolling field dominated their second picture. The glow attracted passing travelers on the highway. The children exited their parents' cars and ran toward the tantalizing crop until the yellows loomed high above, a dark nexus at their center. They entered the field. Light dimmed and luminous shades disappeared, leaving only dank earth, humid undergrowth, and thin sky-blue shards poking through a leafy canopy.

Lost in strangling hues—Forest Green, Asparagus, and Fern—they retreated and abandoned their second drawing.

In a desk that occupied a small nook beside the kitchen, Susu found what they needed to uncover yellow's unbridled essence: three shimmering highlighters.

"Rapeseed will be friendlier," he said.

The children didn't draw a crop but a glare. All three had been mesmerized by blinding yellow fields each spring, manifesting earth's pure energy. Tallis, Janiel, and Susu kept their heads above the blooms as they explored incandescent fields. Reflected light glimmered upon their faces. They became the most important sentences in the textbook of life.

The completed art resembled fluorescent yellow paper, floodlit from behind, kissed by sunbeams. It radiated as much texture, vibrance, and emotion as an exploding star.

When it was time to play outside, the children floated in brilliant warm bubbles that transformed the landscape.

Two Places at Once

A man can be where he is
and where he is not.

A magician is pulling a rabbit out
of his hat while that same rabbit
merrily munches a carrot in its cage,

Traffic outside,
every car home in its garage.

Boy holding hands, with the freckled girl,
with his GI Joe.

I kiss you on the lips the same moment
I kiss my grandmother on the cheek.

People of the inner city, do you hear
the wolf howl as I do?
Creatures of the deep woods,
sorry if the cries
of starving children disturb you,

A man is silent with himself
while talking to his neighbors.
He's regretting
what he's done
though he hasn't done it yet.

Today is at least one other day,
maybe two.
Tomorrow for example.
And the day after.
You can even throw in yesterday.

Crossroads

She said she was
from all over.
I was from one place.

And she'd had
all kinds of jobs
from waitress to
cleaning motel rooms.
I'd been at a desk,
in a cubicle,
all my working years.

So she was ready
to settle down
in the one location,
at the one task.
While I had this
great urge
to be on the move,
do many different things.

So we met momentarily
in a bar,
both about to live the life
the other had been living.

We never saw each other again.
Except in the mirror that is.

January Love

I'm sorry he died when the weather was bad.
Who wants to stand out in a cemetery
in sleet and snow where temperature is the mad king
and all of his minions are frozen and irrelevant.
And yet my mother is angry
that the funeral is so poorly attended.
This is the bitter cold of January.
The geese are still around.
I can see their shadows swoop through mine.
The marsh is clouded up
like my mind when I try to think too deeply,
as if my opinion could possibly mean anything
And these are days
of ice-locked land in all directions,
coated with light that can go no deeper.
There's a dead a man in the ground
and, in the cold and stillness of my blood,
my future is simple—
I am no longer a father's son.
The winter gives pause,
makes me doubt the ability of vegetation to renew.
I have seen what bitterness does to people
My mother's eyes are still capable of welling up.
But that's for what has been,
not for how things are now.
I am witnessing the beginning of widowhood.
It parallels the month in so many ways.
The geese don't migrate. They hang around.
They've figured out how to live with the worst.
They feed and drink where they can.
My mother even tosses bread to them.
Not good for their bodies, so I've heard,
but wonderful for their souls.

Life and Death

I have always been on good terms with my doctor. Russell and I understand each other. As a master hypochondriac, I have used my medical education to conjure up some truly arcane and sometimes charmingly quaint threats to my well being. Journeymen hypochondriacs worry about strokes or cancer; I tend more toward yaws or pinta or leishmaniasis. Some doctors would be annoyed by my bottomless need for reassurance, but Russell finds my sense of doom entertaining. He doesn't complain about getting paid for his work, but I am grandiose enough to suspect that, in my case, the money is just a bonus.

It was with this history in mind that Russell responded to the message about the arrhythmia. I had been sitting in my office taking my pulse (even apprentice hypochondriacs know that one) and noticed that it was irregular. I felt fine at the time, no symptoms of any kind, unless you count compulsively taking my pulse as a symptom. It was what doctors call an incidental finding. Still, you can't be too careful; I called Russell.

At the end of his day, he called me back. He spoke in that voice you use to tell your child that, yes, there are bad people in the world, but we aren't going to let you get kidnapped. He reminded me of the usual preliminary steps we would normally go through to evaluate this finding—physical exam, EKG, treadmill test—and he told me that we both knew that if they were all negative, I still wouldn't be satisfied, so he suggested we go right to a Holter monitor. A Holter monitor is a device about the size of a paperback book that you carry around for twenty-four hours while it records your heart rhythm. Then a computer scans the entire record and prints up a report.

I stopped by after work on Monday to get hooked up, and then I dropped the gadget off at the end of the day on Tuesday. Late Wednesday morning Russell called me.

"The Holter results just came in. They are concerning. You have to go to the hospital." "Concerning" is a medical euphemism for "alarming." I said okay, and asked when he thought I should do that. I told him I'd be done in the office at five o'clock, but I imagined he'd say the next morning would be fine.

"No, now. You have to go now."

Russell is not an alarmist; he is not even a concernist. So I was out the door and on my way to the hospital. It is a curious event when a black belt hypochondriac finds out something is seriously wrong. You would think I would have been prepared. The fact was, I felt cheated; all that worrying in advance had failed to inoculate me against disaster.

I arrived at the hospital and signed forms. After an exhaustive diagnostic assessment of my insurance and finances, I was admitted—to the Intensive

Care Unit. I think that took me aback almost as much as being sent to the hospital at all. I had just spent maybe two hours doing routine paperwork, and now they were saying I needed to be monitored every second. It was as if I had to apply for a bank loan first, and then they would stop the bleeding. Even more disorienting was the fact that at no time had I felt at all unwell.

Once I was deprived of my clothes, put to bed, and hooked up to a cardiac monitor, Russell came in with another man whom he introduced as Dr. Strane. He was to be my cardiologist. Dr. Strane went over the Holter results with me and I got the message what the alarm—excuse me, concern—was all about. The main point was that I had had several runs of ventricular tachycardia, each lasting for twenty or more beats. I had enough cardiology background to ask and have Dr. Strane confirm that 80 percent of people with "nonsustained runs of v-tach" die suddenly within five years of diagnosis.

On other occasions of illness, I had noted that my awareness had tended to split in two. On one side, I was sick and immersed in being small and helpless and (ideally) looked after by mothers and their ilk. On the other side, I was fascinated by the pathophysiology and science and technology. But no previous illness had been life threatening. On this occasion, my awareness split in a different way. I had no interest in the whirlwind of diagnostic tests and procedures; I let myself be poked and scanned and echoed as if I weren't quite inhabiting my body. But on the other, I was trying to make sense out of something that, despite my hypochondriasis, I had never seriously considered: I was going to die.

For the next two days, I had an echocardiogram, an MRI, a thallium stress test, and I don't remember what else. On day three, I was scheduled to have an angiogram, but before that happened, Dr. Strane came in to talk to me. He told me he had consulted with Mel Scheinman, the director of the electrophysiology lab at the University of California San Francisco, who was the expert in these kinds of arrhythmias. Scheinman had said that there was a subtype of v-tach that was benign, which accounted for the 20 percent that survived. There was a simple, noninvasive test that would identify the subtype. It was called a signal-averaged EKG, and he thought we should try that before doing an angiogram. We did, and it turned out that I had the benign variant.

I was discharged the same day, with no medication, no treatment, no need for follow-up. I was officially fine. I felt as if I had been abducted by aliens for their experiments and then summarily beamed back down to my cornfield, where I stood blinking and confused.

Beyond the immense relief of a narrow escape, I found myself feeling cheated again. I had barely had time to notice that I was dying, and now it wasn't the case. But, of course, I was wrong. The question of my dying was never an "if." For two days, I felt as if I had been granted a glimpse at my own mortality, but without the time to learn from it. Now I had the time back, and

I knew—I *knew!*—I was going to die, even if I didn't know when, and I was sure there was treasure in that knowledge, if only I could mine it.

But somehow it kept slipping away. Over the next few weeks, it felt less and less real—or more accurately, more and more familiar. The memory was transforming itself from an eye-opening, life-altering experience to another dinner conversation. I could not hold onto it.

It is now twenty years since Russell's phone call. Russell died eight years ago from an unexpected heart attack. Dr. Strane has retired. I met Dr. Scheinman once since, to confirm that no follow-up was indicated. He warned me how some people organize their lives around being cardiac patients, and he advised me to get on with my life. He did not know me the way Russell did. I have gotten on with it, and I am no less a hypochondriac now than I was then, although, curiously, I find that I don't worry about my heart. The one lingering effect of the whole ordeal is that I still feel that, somehow, it was an opportunity lost.

Speaking Through the Silence

—after "Message," painting by Lois Tarlow

Finally the painting whispers to me
words I've long tried to hear. It says
this darkness is not absolute.
A starless night holds within it
certainty of morning, promise of light,
the silent rush of an owl's wing,
singing of breeze through dry brush,
soft intake of breath before speech.

It says even in silence people can reach
each other. Figures drawn on a wall:
This is a deer, this a hunter. This is what
it says to me with these sticks and shapes.
I look at what the artist has painted,
in wonder at the language she speaks.

Bamboo

In the gentle evening air,
the bamboo is stirring.

It is not streaming like the tawny manes
of warhorses flowing over the steppe,
nor like the scarlet banners of their riders.

It is not rippling like a pond brushed
with breeze, nor thrashing
like the famished North Sea in February.

It is not fluttering like the corps de ballet,
nor waving like a crowd on the pier
as a great ship eases out of the harbor.

In lengthening shadows, the bamboo
is moving like bamboo.

Guests

Surprise: a late night knocking at the door.
It's my parents, all dressed up for traveling,
Father with his fedora. They're looking well,
and younger than before. *May we come in?*
I step aside. Though glad to see them,
I wonder what has brought them here.
Is something wrong? But no:
Since you no longer come to visit us,
we thought we'd better visit you.
The trip was long, and now we're tired.
We need to rest a while. I point them
toward the guest room, *make yourselves at home,*
then follow with a quiet broom,
cleaning up the clay they've trailed behind.

Athenian Holiday

Heat, toxic smog and mobs
of tourists and refugees—
the city, as always, lives
up to its reputation.

Mornings in godforsaken shrines
whitened by time's slow bleach.
Inscriptions treading back and forth:
oxen plowing a field.

Museums in blazing afternoons,
a surfeit of vases and weapons
marking the ages of mankind:
stone, bronze, iron.

Nights in that modest hotel
on Bouboulinas Street
where the ghosts of the tortured
still wander, wordless.

The Doom of Heroes

Ten years, and it all led up to this.

The evening of the series finale of *Game of Thrones* found me in Cape Cod with two of my closest friends. Gathering around the laptop with glasses of wine, snacks, and somewhat cautious expectations, we hopped onto HBO to let the games begin. We took bets on who would be the first character to go, and while all around agreeing it would be a "Shakespearian" ending; everyone would die. But we never thought the *entire series* would die like this.

Our enthusiasm dropped by the minute. A chorus of "What?" "Why?" and "I feel like I'm not even watching the same show anymore," sounded through the room. Nothing made sense. The world had fallen into chaos. None of us could sleep that night, and hashed and rehashed everything that had gone wrong the next day. Even at Cape Cod, the sun was a little dimmer; the world had grown a little darker. I looked out across the ocean and watched that dragon fly away along with all hope for some sense of closure.

That was the day heroes died.

Nearly two years have passed since the end of *Game of Thrones*. The dust has settled, the people have spoken. The fans, the actors, and George R.R. Martin himself have weighed in on the topic. A now-infamous petition came and went, demanding HBO rewrite the most controversial and troubled season in *Game of Thrones* history. Although the petition picked up steam amongst fans, caught the notice of some notable *Game of Thrones* actors, and even the show-runners themselves, it was never taken very seriously by anyone except those who signed it … including me. I felt moved to put my name to this subtle protest after watching a program that had come to underscore the last ten years of my life go down in a flaming wreck along with King's Landing; the strongest women in an internationally renowned fantasy series were ultimately left speechless. Last spring, during lockdown due to the COIVD-19 pandemic, HBO posted on social media encouraging viewers to watch the show from beginning to end once more. What a backlash! Many responses to HBO's post should never be repeated in polite company.

Back in May of 2019, I was splitting my time into thirds: as a writer, a mother, and an English Instructor in higher education. As an instructor, I spent a good deal of time discussing the Hero's Journey. The Hero's Journey has always been with us, from Achilles to Hercules, to Harry Potter and Moana. Each hero begins in the ordinary world … what life is like for him or her before they begin their adventure. *Game of Thrones* very obviously followed two main characters from the very start as they began their journey. It was about Jon Snow and Daenerys Targaryen. Jon's journey began in the ordinary world of Winterfell and Daenerys in her brother's keeping. There was a call to action:

leaving Winterfell/heading out with Kahl Drogo. There was the refusal of the call, the "I can't do it" moment, but the hero/heroine went on to meet the mentor and crossed the threshold into the unknown. There were tests, there were meetings of allies and enemies. There was an ordeal where the hero died (getting stabbed by friends or being burned alive in a funeral pyre would do), but they came back more determined than ever. They seized a special weapon—Jon's sword, Daenerys's dragons—and headed back home ready to confront the enemy for the last time.

At this very crucial point in the hero's journey, there was a final confrontation with the enemy. They faced certain death but used everything in their arsenal of knowledge gained along the way … and *should* have come out victorious and returned home with some sort of gift for the world. Liberation, enlightenment, knowledge. The problem with *Game of Thrones* was that neither Jon nor Daenerys returned with a gift of knowledge. They didn't enlighten anyone; they didn't liberate anyone. The writers of *Game of Thrones* failed at a critical point which, as a writer myself, felt glaringly wrong. Jon gained absolutely no knowledge (I must say this once: "You know nothing, Jon Snow.") and Daenerys died without becoming the liberator she so long dreamed of becoming. Daenerys's liberation of King's Landing turned into a senseless slaughter which was *forcibly created* to justify her ultimate betrayal and death, a case of 1+1=3. The heroes failed on their journey, and as I once told my students, those who do not complete the hero's journey are doomed to repeat it. Bye, Jon Snow. Back to the wall with ye.

There were several other problems with the two final episodes in the last season of *Game of Thrones:* a slapdash ending that looked like it was written ten minutes before it aired, failure to complete character arcs and backslides on character evolution, a problem with the passage of time, plot points that dropped off into the ether, prophecies unfulfilled, liberal borrowing from *Star Wars* (Darth Daenerys anyone?) and an overall sense of absolute disappointment that left my friends and me confused and depressed for days.

But I digress.

As a mother and a woman, I objected to both Daenerys's and Cersei's silent demise, not at the hands of falling bricks or those they loved, but by writers who assassinated their characters and silenced their spirits. Daenerys's character was identifiable to many women who could see themselves reflected in her: someone who had been abused and betrayed, suffered the loss of a child, and struggled to make her way in a world dominated by men. Those she cared for the most betrayed her, and her lover quite literally stuck a knife in her heart. Cersei, although much less likable, was also someone we could identify with. Her anticlimactic ending at a handful of falling bricks silenced a woman who could have, and would have, gone out swinging in any other scenario.

What *was* it about the world in 2019, that felt a need to silence strong women? Why did men dominate, degrade, call women hysterical, power-hungry, crazy, mad, or nasty? What was the moral to the story here, the lesson passed on to our daughters, those little girls named Daenerys, Cersei, and even Sansa and Arya over the last ten years? What has *Game of Thrones* taught us? That women cannot be successful rulers? I found much of the year's political climate reflected in that last episode, considering a man who spent much of his time doing nothing at all claimed the kingship of Westeros. This was where I agreed with the petition; the fault lay with the writers. Two men, left on their own to finish a plot where Martin's original storyline left off, created pin-up girls doomed to fail. Women writers were needed to create strong heroines, not just pin-up girls, but *heroines* who put aside the men who failed them in search of a better truth.

There have been many types of heroes. There have been anti-heroes, willing heroes, and yes, even tragic heroes. Think Shakespeare's *Othello* for a prime example of a tragic hero. Othello killed his wife thinking she had betrayed him. When he discovered the truth of her innocence, he killed himself because he couldn't live with that guilt. Although he died, he attained knowledge, completed his journey, and reached his end. Perhaps Jon Snow should have admitted he knew nothing. Perhaps Daenerys should have flown straight for the Red Keep and took Cersei down … a much more fulfilling end than a pile of bricks. So many things *should* have happened that it boggles the mind.

In October of 2019, I found myself back at Cape Cod, thinking about the dragon flying off over the ocean. If I looked hard enough, I could still see the shape of dark wings on the horizon, and what I felt was a strange sense of purpose. For if I had reacted to the doom of heroes with so much passion and outrage, so have hundreds if not thousands of writers, instructors, students, mothers … women across the world. The doom of our heroes pushed us to take to the sky. The failure to complete the journey put a pen in our hands. Now, two years after the fall of King's Landing, we have seen heroines rise from the ashes of Daenerys and Cersei in both fiction and in real life. Rey Skywalker. Kamala Harris. Women to whom my seven-year-old daughter looks up to with pride and hope and truth shining in her eyes. Women who have written a better ending. Women who have broken the wheel.

One Thin Wall

One thin wall divided the single-wide
into what they called a cozy two bedroom.

One thin wall fractured the home
each time a fist or phone flew through.

One thin wall that shook the trailer
when a body was thrown against it

unless it's a full bottle night and the force
finds an adult in the children's room.

One thin wall patched into a plaid—the checked
pattern reminiscent of a full body cast.

Delivery

Because the patient gives me the wrong address—
because when I call my manager, she tells me
keep searching—I sprint with cheesy tortellini
down eleven dim flights, cursing broken
elevators. On the ground floor Panera
calls again and asks *where are you?* I say
in the hospital. After silence, I clarify—*for
a customer*—and she tells me *who you seek
is next door.* I lament the time I wasted
driving this black bag in a small vessel
to the wrong drop-off, and even more, time
spent walking from one mistake to the next.
Hospital lights hue everything sickly.
What is it I am trying to deliver? I look
through the inventory of my belongings
and, after the hand-off, bear the lightness.

Ingrained

Pillow wheat, it wakens
underneath overalls
and field boots, beaten

by the harvesting dredge
of a man in sweat, sun
beating down his setting.

It is summer, and he
holds a scythe, slicing heads
with curvaceous blade

to make a maelstrom
of land mattress, to quake
folds of fibrous gold.

He molds a pot of arms,
reaching into riches,
his horde of heavy work.

He refuses to rinse
fingers, instead fitting
his wealth, germinated.

Instructions from a Ferry

I watch a television through a reflection
in a dirty mirror:

How to inflate a lifesaving flotation device.

I shrink to age 12, when my sister first told me
I hope you die during an argument.

We cried while my mother drove, scared I would
be dead by the day's end.

*Do not try to help other passengers
before you've helped yourself.*

It's been 9 years, and some days I think
she wishes me dead as her nightly prayer.

In the very unlikely case of emergency,

I feel like a fraud dressed in the skin of
an adult. I wish my mother would call
and tell me she misses me,
I wish my sister would tell my father
she loves him and mean it.

Do not panic. Proceed to the nearest

I wish I could be sure of one fucking thing
without my head going sideways,
& my brain melting out my ears.

exit.

I wish for peace, because my mother needs it
more than the rest of us,
because my dad is poor with emotions,
because my sister inherited an inability to be kind.

Because I love what's around me,
but the boat I'm on makes it impossible to see
out the window at night,
and I'm left staring at the reflection of the t.v.

From all of us aboard, have a safe and relaxing trip.

Five Haiku

The Climb

Climbing without hands,
Wilderness of astral blue.
Upward a plane's wings fly.

Dreams

A moment, a thought,
Hope's peaceful meditation,
Embraces the now.

Time

The clock ticks then tocks,
Strolls the avenues of time,
Circle of eternity.

Idaho

A farmer's open plain.
Claim to fame, Appaloosas,
Long roads, potatoes.

Prayer

Listen to me, God!
How often do I listen?
Listen means silent.

Testy Waters

(an acrostic)

Fishing off a pier in summer shower
Red cork pelted by the falling rain
Every now and then the float will move
Seems like there might be a bite or nibble
Have no shelter from the wind today
Wettened already head to toe
As the hour extends to four p.m.
Tugging on the line, no doubt about it
Every second's timing crucial now
Reel in as the bobber disappears

Line tightens and rod bends
Is it a bass, a catfish, or something else?
Temptation is to try to horse it in
Exceptional fight put up by this fish
Reel out a little line and let it run
Able to tire it out a little bit
Ratchet down to medium line drag
Yes, now it's coming in but slowly

Jumbo catfish on the other end
Only have to give it a bit more slack
Underneath the water it is thrashing
Reach out with the net when it breaks surface
Never try to hoist it onto the boards
Almost got it now, just a bit closer
Long arm fully proffered, catch secured

Climate Survival

The issue of the millennium smolders
beneath the distractions of the political
climate rife with corruption, and denial
remains constant, a system of high
pressure more constant than prayer.
Needing to look away, I cast my gaze
through the streaked office window.

Finches, whose tiny bodies sway on
spent mustard stalks, peck at the pods
until the seeds are exposed. There is
enough for now and a few spill away,
like an offering to Mother Earth so
she may again grant the mustard's return.
Taking flight, the finches are a blur
of mustard sunshine. Will they survive
the growing fire of our making?

Sun Shower

Drinking from a glass
Of ice-cold water, I
Take delight in the after-
Noon sun shower as
It fills the bird bath drop
By drop like fingers tapping
Single notes on the piano;
The music wakes a solitary bee
From his drunken pollen
Stupor in a squash blossom
And sputters to find his way
Back to the hive, a trail of
ephemeral sweetness before
being absorbed once again
into the sun and soil.

Sherman, TX 1988

Like much of my history
I have forgotten his name.
He arrived daily at the office
around 3:45 to meet
his girlfriend, a sweet middle-
aged woman whose name
I also can't recall, and waited
in the corner of the lobby
not in deference but politeness
with the calm of a man accustomed
to being judged.

He was old enough to be
my father, uncle, or mentor.
Gravity had pulled his features
and laid bare a sadness his clothes
could not disguise.
He always wore a suit
buttoned against the stifling Texas
heat. Insouciantly, he examined
his jacket for lint or a wayward thread
His tie remained perfectly
centered and pulled tight
against his collar as though
it might choke him.

Our conversation never moved
beyond polite pleasantries like
the weather or the Texas Rangers,
but before all of that I asked
how he made his living. He said
he was an attorney in town, the first
Black lawyer since the lynchings. His
voice low with the resolve of a man
unwilling to be defeated. A living
monument to courage and the human
spirit worthy of being set in bronze.

Demands

I want to tie a scarf around my head and someone to lead me to a table and chair. On the table will be a cake, a cake with white frosting and small blue triangles around the circumference. Someone will hand me a fork and I'll start eating. It will taste better than any cake I've eaten before. The fork won't suffice. I'll put it down and grab at the cake with my hands, stuffing fistfuls into my mouth. Crumbs will scatter across the table, fall to my lap, the floor. Icing will get caught in the corners of my mouth and stick to my fingers. If the blindfold slips, I will have to push it up with the backs of my hands. Normally, I would mind. Little will remain of the cake. I won't be bothered by the blindfold, but I'll regret eating the cake. I'll wish instead for someone to lay me down, to read me a story, to listen to the rise and fall of their voice.

Algorithmic Heart

I never really understood how the Bacon
number worked, how Kevin was so close
to Chaplin. You told me Tippi Hedren
starred in *Marnie*, some film about a woman
who mistrusted men and froze at the sight
of the color red.

Typing actors into the screen is pointless,
in a way. Like the time I didn't come home,
too saturated with vodka to care about you.
I wanted to see the stars with her,
to determine the shape of the universe.

You were always too cold in the night,
and even when I offered my warmth,
you polarized us through Doppler
effect—the spectra of our bodies shifting
red then blue.

Do I look as old as he does?

dinner in a bar
on the river
in carrick-on-shannon
on my father's
60th birthday. 60 years old,
and looking
about 60,
he takes the chance
to hold court,
to have wine
and some three pints
of guinness. on the walls
are photos of politicians
and actors eating,
and musicians.
he points to each one
in wide beery candour,
says "do I look old
as he does?" we eat together,
looking at our steaks
and potatoes,
his teetotal
leitrim neighbours
patient as they listen
to him drinking.

If only I'd been a painter

days on the days
and also their years,
and I thought of nothing
but sky and its opening—
its red light, its dark
and its melancholy. I thought of it
much as water
in a glass must think
of the glass, as unread books
must think of the shelf
they sit upon. the rose
rising westward
as the sun fell through
and burned the air
to thunderstorm. the bearing lines
of highways, as they humped
their cargos up. the texture
of my wallpaper, blue
shading to black
and purple. I lay back
on the sofa,
eating toast and staring
through the windows. god,
stretched on a long
workday, legs
to the horizon, flaming
a blue distance—the colours
and their autumn
blues.

Accident

If only it had not rained
the sky black and wet as
we hurried across streets.

Perhaps had he worn a
light coat it would have
been easier to spot.

Maybe if the cab driver
were not so tired, if
headlights shone brighter.

How many hundreds of things
lead him to that corner.
For instance staying late
to check computer printouts.

The cab driver had felt like
going home at six but had
a recent rent increase.

Everything lead to the cab
slipping along 3rd Avenue.
Him in front of his office
and then lunging out to
avoid a puddle.

There was no one to blame
nothing to blame really
not the rain
or the dark coat
not the dim lights
nor the cab driver
who would remember this always
and sometimes blame himself.

It was part of a series
of events of time and place
leading to this conclusion.

An ambulance screamed
down the avenue. His eyes
wide open as he lay
facing the black night.

His time finished
eyes opened as if
staring at something
quite different now.

Holding Firmer by Roots Through Her Trunk

She crashed down
on oak leafed ground,
stayed a long, long while
before deciding to die, made sounds
whether or not humans heard.
Ripped by winds and weakened by rains
this forty tall white oak declined.
Roots had grown around large rocks underground
pulling them into the light, holding them close.
Roots, just naked branches, bark-less, had stretched
slowly, pushing through sand and soil,
searching like water witches,
tunneling like miners for real wealth,
dried out by salted breezes, sun-burnt,
withered, fell off.
All else gave up, blew away.

But three twigs sought sun,
their own roots from mother bark cloned,
created to pierce the dying trunk,
speared ground below,
slowly pushing through xylem and phloem,
growing upward as mother had before,
smooth barked, leafed, now tall and thick,
held firmer by roots through the old one.
The sun-side trunk lived long enough,
twigs realigned their destiny with gravity, and
re-created.

Ode to an Oriole

Your feet and claws, nothing like my needles,
your beak doesn't resemble my crochet hook,
but your nest reminds me of my knitted blanket
I spent months on. In less time, you completed
an avian opus, hanging from a branch, of strength
and flexibility, outside my porch.

I couldn't have learned from others unless
some wise woman once watched your techniques,
skill and determination. I may be driven
by the same instincts to warm my babies, soften my home
with fibers, where we sit and observe what we don't
understand: the maple your mate selected,
neighborhood near fruit and an insect supermarket,
trees and waters acceptable to both of us.

And we do our thing with
moss and grass outdoors,
fibers and fabrics inside,
until satisfied for a season.

My hands are taught by your
feet and beak, in active meditation
on what warms and protects. We, too, migrate
to be closer to the salty ocean in winter,
then return to produce what we must,
on slightly wooded plains in sun
and warm summer breezes,
waiting for our creative
knotting to wear out
and be replaced
by more,
and more.

Time Curves

Winter plumage confuses identification.
Loons, with their cry that bows the soul's strings,
transform from the most elegant feathering:
black head, neck and dagger-beak, white throat band,
checkered black and white markings on the back.
They met and mated on inland lakes, nested and nurtured
in one season that takes us a score of years, then
transformed in parting to the coasts.
They turn gray, beak to tail,
all shadowed in shallows along the coasts,
like rock stars who don Trapist Robes, vow celibacy,
still singing the hours in beauty but
hooded in meditative colorlessness.
I gray too after decades of wild exploration to find one mate,
settling onto land and raising our brood, in our own nest we built.
But my time is linear, my living headed towards shadows.
Loons live my life annually, shed the gray feathers,
polish the beak that blackens brilliantly,
ready for breeding again in the Spring.
They return home, flying above the curvature of earth,
start over with mates,
breed, build, nest and nourish.
I have no more eggs to roll down tubes, ready to meet the wiggling
other half of our humanity. But I keep my mate as I'm kept.
We travel through time linearly, growing more alike as we age.
Loons live a spiral existence, variations
on a percussive rhythm that generates seasonally.
Gray to brilliance, to gray to brilliance.

Egret

A sun so bright it seems
To burn blue from air,
While here, by tidal waters,
A vivid plume of cloud- Melt, a buoy's body,
Legs as thin as the
Shafts of a compass
And a face that's fused
With the sensuous neck.
The head now appears
Too far ahead of its body
As it leans to surface,
Patient as a muse,
Hunched until instinct
Compels the quick,
Lyrical thrust of bill,
Like a piston fired,
Whistles thru the water's
Canopy of olive-
Green bladder-wrack
Neon shimmer
Extinguished in
Single swallow
And the lethal
Gaze soon returns
To water, much
The way memory
Might pause in
Pursuit of color,
Touch or voice.

Homestead

Ghostly birds drifting lazily to air,
Like a fragrance that's been
Eased from earth and holds near
To this day's downfallen heaven.

A few, solitary clouds appear
In sun-silvered drift, blend
Into a smoke-like feathering
That wreathes the horizon.

The house, too, seems prepared
To drift and I also sense
It's loose, untethered stairs
Would rise and extend

Up into this basin of rare,
Pearl-blue sky where they'd bend,
Bearing the all of it, towards the nearer
Stars aglint, arcing in perilous ascent.

Preserved

An intricate necklace adorns the lake,
Its combed strands of pearled white
Advancing earth, though the center
Pulp softly churns. The ice makes
For a half-healed and lightless
Surface. The cold reassures;
An after-life gray will overtake
The lake's receding brightness
And still the far interior.

Random, pendant flakes
Adrift in tangled flight;
They rise, fall, linger
And seem to congregate
Like moths in mid-air despite
A sudden down-rush
Of wind. All's in a state
Of snow-bright darkness
Never knowing, for sure,

If light's a thing let in or out.

437 Wilton Street (A Brick Story)

Charlie's wistful heart tingles as he pulls up to 437 Wilton Street, the apartment building from his childhood. Everything is gone but the skeleton of a structure and the echoes of Charlie's memories. You can board up the windows, but you can't cross out the souls that once occupied the walls.

Every Saturday night, the entire block would light up with a Fourth of July jubilance. Dueling music speakers battled to steal the humid air at full volume. The Ramones shouted to the rooftop. Bruce Springsteen crooned to the moon. And Sam Cooke sang to the heavens.

Out in the street, Rich used to show off his candy red Mustang. Rich thought he was a lot cooler than he actually was. His hair grease looked like a mixture of egg yolks and cement. Charlie hasn't forgotten the time that Rich revved up his ride in front of the whole neighborhood, only to blow the engine. As everybody laughed, Rich's face blushed redder than his broken car.

Shawn was the tallest human that Charlie had ever seen. He dribbled the basketball on the bubblegum-stained concrete like he had the world in his hands. He never did make it to the pros, though. But he did become a pro of another kind. Charlie hadn't heard about Shawn in years until the day a familiar voice spoke through the television. It was a commercial for a landscaping business—aptly named Shawn's Professional Landscaping.

Charlie wished that he were older. Then, maybe he might've gotten noticed by his first crush, Henrietta. He'd often daydream about her curly hair, sparkly lip gloss, and mysterious eyes. Sometimes when Charlie passed by her door, he'd hear loud yelling and harsh bangs. Wherever she is now, he hopes that she's safe and happy.

TJ always treated Charlie like a little brother. He'd even give him extra cash for snacks every single week. Charlie always admired TJ's bright red Nike shoes. One day, TJ got arrested by the cops in front of Charlie's very own eyes. It turned out that TJ was selling a certain kind of product, and it wasn't chocolates.

Charlie's grandma cooked the most delicious spaghetti. It smelled like love. The sauce was made from fresh tomatoes that she grew on the building's rooftop. Charlie still thinks of her sweet smile with the missing front tooth, and the big, dark moles on her cheeks. The cancer eventually got to her. When she was put to rest, Charlie was forced to go into a new home. But it wasn't really a home. The memories from that place are the ones that Charlie permanently boarded up in his mind.

After snapping out of his trance, Charlie picks up a decrepit brown brick from the building and sets it on the passenger side floor of his pristine Cadillac. When he arrives back at his quaint house in a quiet neighborhood, he places the brick in the soil of his tomato garden and smiles.

Rearranged

My living room was always wrong you see.
Every month to my husband's dismay,
I moved all the furniture tirelessly.
Pacing, I'd imagine a better way.

Thinking this time, I would get it perfect.
But everything we owned was not mine.
Hand-me-downs and things I didn't select.
I wasn't at home with what was assigned.

All this time I swallowed the truth at hand:
Husband was malicious, life felt so grim.
Of course my home felt like a stranger's land.
No rearrangement could solve that problem.

I was restless and deep down, knew the source
But moving chairs was simpler than divorce.

Hard to Swallow

The food won't go down.
It turns to poison
in my mouth.
Unsafe intrusion.
Heart beating too fast.

I spit into the trash.
Forcing up anything
that started to enter
my esophagus.
I drink a Diet Coke instead.

I get back into bed
I touch my hip bones
and my ribs,
A meditation. Safe again.
My hunger still intact.

The Wedding Dress

What excitement! I thought my days were over. But here I am. I have just been purchased on eBay for Jennifer's wedding. At least I will be out of this house of despair. I actually like Jim, but Karen leaves a lot to be desired. I was worn at their wedding reception when Karen's mother insisted upon having a post-wedding reception at their Golf course country clubhouse in the Garden of the Gods. I was picked off the rack impulsively, I think as Karen's mother did not approve of the other dress choices that Karen liked. Sure, I was traditional, very lacey, Victorian, pale champagne and tea length so I could be worn again.

No, Karen was not going to choose a white-white dress after sleeping with Jim for six months as well as several other eligible men before that. But Jim loved her, his mother liked her, even giving up her widow's diamond for their engagement ring. I really liked the reception, photos from every angle and lots of celebration. I certainly played my role of making Karen look good. Strange there was no alcohol served at the reception. A party is always more fun and livelier with at least champagne and wine flowing. Religious restriction, I guessed.

But when Karen and Jim got home, she let her guard down. What frustration it must have been, no alcohol for 72 hours. All those AA and Alateen meetings and counseling with her parents. What good were they? So, no alcohol at the wedding was probably a sign to her parents friends and relatives that surely Karen was "cured. "

Jim did not mind a drink or two. A nice glass of wine before the elaborate dinners she wooed him with even relaxed him. However, as the months rolled along and I hung in the closet of their apartment, I could hear the bickering after dinner about who was supposed to keep the house clean and why could she not have at least a cocktail before dinner. Karen would get up at night and have a few shots of whiskey to avoid Jim's suggestions on how to cut back on her drinking. No, he would not have another glass of wine, there was no reason to rush through the bottle.

I did get out to several parties that they both enjoyed. One was his holiday company dance and another a wedding of her workmate. I certainly looked nice and enjoyed being dropped to the floor when they got home and were hungry for sex. But back into the closet I went in the morning, but I could still hear them and see her as she chose what to wear to work that day.

But the conversations accelerated into arguments and then when he was away on business, she would choose me to hit the casino down the street. Hour after hour we sat playing those slots; she accepting the free drinks every hour she continues to sit there. I was beginning to smell like smoke and booze combined. She never had me cleaned but I was happy that she chose me to go out.

Then one day Jim did not come home. Sure, there was plenty of arguments over the phone and I could see the divorce coming. Other wedding dresses I knew were packed away after only one wearing as the couple began having kids. Other dresses were pulled out and offered to a daughter or daughter-in-law to wear and I even heard of one woman who wanted to be buried in the most beautiful dress she ever owned.

Seemed that money was tight, so one day Karen took me to the bridal shop and tried to consign me. "No," said the clerk, "this dress is out of style and pretty well worn." I think she was trying to be polite as I smelled like a barroom. So, for a quarter of what her mother paid for me, I was placed on eBay. Interesting that someone would bid on something you can't try on. But sure, enough for $45. Jennifer won me and I am on my way by Fed Ex to her home hopefully with a happier existence, even if just one more party.

Reaching for the Flying Plum

If I sit still and ground myself like a tree
I can almost imagine heartwood in flight—

Unbound by bedrock or soil, roots quivering on bare sky,
Tobiume, the flying plum of Japanese lore

Soaring all the way from Kyoto to Fukuoka
Hundreds of miles to rejoin its favorite human

The exiled scholar Michizane—because no garden
Can hold back what sun blesses free and fierce.

Tobiume's legend sprouted over a millennia ago, but
I still hear the flutter and billow of each branch,

White petals flowering like a thousand times
A thousand stories of sacred stars, and I too enshrine

Bright shades of leaf and bud in my heart for those
Hours I fall without wings, yet dare on a dream,

On breath and breeze—blood and sap draw
Strength even under strange blue and wild airs.

Super Bloom

Sometimes I shrivel and fall to the eighth lowest
Place in the world, down to Death Valley

In the summer of 1913 when the ground
Simmered and crackled at 134 degrees—
The hottest day ever recorded by man.
I feel the sear inside me now, every hue and hope

Puffing into cinder dreams deep within dead sands
Until I'm certain I'll never know lush colors again
Not *understand* tinge and glow even if I could slake
My own soul-parched eyes with life one more time.

But the sky remembers even if I forget myself,
Falling in a perfect storm in the valley just over
A century later, a mere one and a half measly inches
Of water bursting barren earth into a rare super bloom—

Yellow armfuls of sun-hearted Desert Gold, tall lace sprigs
Of white Gravel Ghost, round blossom heads of Purple
Sand Verbena, nosegays of bell-shaped Notch Phacelia,
And scarlet beauty marks of pink-blushing Desert Fivespot.

I cast the promise of these petals against my mental aridity,
Tearing seeds with earnest moisture—patient orbs I plant

For the century, or the second, of my own super bloom.

Synestia Moon

Once upon a synestia,

Two planets collided in the young dark
Bright of space and vaporized each other.

The wild ruins of Earth and Theia whirled anew
Into a spinning ring rich with molten matter.

Droplets tamed by gravity rained inwards,
Condensing the hot new heart of the world.

But a globe escaped the sear of this birthing storm,
Cooling into an orb with a face not far from pearl.

For the briefest snatch of time, the moon's surface
Gleamed smooth and unbroken, suspended like a dream

No human eyes would ever see before meteor scarred,
Pocked, and cratered lunar symmetry out of perfection.

But true form and flaw are never beyond imagining—
What the universe forgets, minds may set aglow again.

Kaleidoscope Eyes

Her eyes were windowpanes, distorting images and changing reflections like the mirror in a fun house. They opened and closed, changed color and shape, a relentless kaleidoscope, mesmerizing and hypnotic and strange.

"Why are you here?" she asked, her eyes radiating, spinning, humming.

He really couldn't say. One minute he was living his comfortable life, the next he was standing before her, transfixed. He had no explanation, no reasoning, nothing made sense. He only knew that this was where he needed to be.

She stared into him, through him. Her eyes opening and closing, spinning and pulsing—vast pinwheels of ever-changing color, they saw everything, felt everything—saw him as he was, for who he was, for who he could be.

"You have to trust me," she said, her eyes shimmering, shining, soothing. "If you fall, I will be there—if you let me."

He stared back, unable to move, unable to breathe, unable to think. Her crazy kaleidoscope eyes held him, comforted him, pulled him in. He was re-minded of a line in a song—*the girl with kaleidoscope eyes*—it was about tripping on LSD. All at once, he was flying, weightless. He was exhilarated and terrified and strangely calm. None of it made sense—he didn't care. He never wanted to leave, never wanted to be far from this feeling, far from her.

"Why are you here?" she asked again, her eyes blue, then green, then tur-quoise, expanding and contracting and changing—always changing.

He still could not answer, which was unusual. He had always lived his life with certainty, clarity, a directness, always a plan. He never took chances, never gambled, but now, as he stood before her, he was dizzy with uncertainty and, at the same time, dizzy with relief. He realized he wanted to live in those eyes forever, never leave.

He focused on a tiny, dried leaf on the ground between them. *I am like that leaf,* he thought to himself, *I am dried up, dead, unable to act. I can be crushed so easily.*

He looked back at her and began to break apart bit by bit. When he was weightless, no longer earthbound, unable to control this roller-coaster ride, she pulled him back in. When she did, *his* eyes began to change—the pupils dilated and constricted, first blue, then purple, then green—endless prisms of light and color radiating outward. He was elated but also afraid.

"You must trust me," she said, her eyes opening and closing, spinning and changing. "If you fall, I will be there—if you let me."

"I can't fall," he said, panic creeping into his voice. "I never want to fall."

"You must let yourself fall a little before you can really fly," she said.

The Great Nursing-Home Escape

Canes, walkers, wheelchairs gathered
casually in the lobby, as if by chance.

A former MIT professor shorted out
the front door alarm with a paperclip.

Distraction was needed. Toilet tissue
on a hotplate brought staff on the run.

Time's prophylactic connivers clanked
out the door, clattered down the drive,

to be swallowed up by accessory oaks,
trees previously acquainted with flight.

Zephyrs retouched grey hair to blond,
blue sky smiled away deep worry-lines.

Look: there were markets, monuments,
entire dimensions the television lacked.

Death shrank to a crow on a trash can,
cawed once, raucous, then flapped off.

Something golden showed beguilingly
beyond the village commons: a future!

All at once, the nursing home minibus
pulled up alongside. It was nearly time

for chicken à la king: they must return.
That golden glow was the setting sun.

Specimen Owl

Docent shows him to children
under the summer-vacation sun.
A cord attaches to one talon.

Injured past chance of survival
in the wild, his life now tweaks
school-age attention deficit.

A chipmunk runs under a bush.
Needless to pounce and clutch:
meals provided free of charge.

His head turns widely; she says
a horned owl's eyes don't move
like ours. No sidelong glances.

To meet his unblinking gaze
is hard for me, one specimen
of an entire suspect species;

off to the side, as becomes
somebody with the wastage
of Eden on his conscience.

These children now scatter
in their transient innocence,
to view, before closing time,

a listless coyote, indifferent
bear, neurotic mountain lion,
one-eyed interned deer.

To the Father Figure Who Didn't Stay

It was a Christmas present,
that orange racket, a gift
from coach to student.
"Hard work," you said,
"should be rewarded."
Too surprised to notice
the paint scraped off
the frame, I saw only
your smile, which gave

no hint that you'd leave
just six months later,
gone without a word,
another chip in the head
of my racket, my grip
unravelling, fatigued,
the tension in my strings

too high. I look for you
even now. I could find you
online, maybe, but what
would I say? And why,
when I can write my own
history for us, something
less final than strings
gone dead—something
less final than the truth?

The Mapmaker

–California, 2020

Pen tight in fist, she draws a map of streets
that wind around the page, swirls of wind
that lift the walls of fire over trees.

Where *Reese's Dairy* stood she draws a box
of blackness, yellow daisies, grass around the box,
draws a blackened chimney—once a house.

Pen tight in fist, she fleshes out her sense
of order, weighs each touch, as if to balance
wear and fear with eye and hand—

I draw my way through smoke, she quips,
quiet the whooshing flames
with loop de loops and jagged lines.

She labors over bush and flourish,
announces *seeds take hold in ash*—

Exit

Approaching forty, Dave Alastair decided it was time to change. He was ready to find a real relationship after years of short but intense flings that always started randomly and ended badly. He was ready to start taking care of his body instead of drinking away his evenings and limiting his exercise routine to weekend softball games. He was ready to try to understand the world around him after following whatever politician wielded the best insults. He was ready to stop blaming his own lack of advancement at work on the people who earned the promotions he thought he deserved.

The night before, Dave decided he was ready to make the effort he had assumed other people were making. He just hadn't been able to commit himself—until now.

Unfortunately, Dave found himself running late for this morning's project-management training session that he decided was the first step toward those life changes he was certain he was ready to make. That's why he took the curving exit ramp leaving Interstate 40 close to twice the posted speed limit. He was annoyed with himself for slightly oversleeping and delaying his new program of self-improvement, and his irritation weighted his heavy foot on the gas pedal. So it was almost a miracle that he was able to stomp on the brake and stop just a dozen yards short of the minivan lying upside-down halfway along the ramp, its front wheel still spinning.

His seatbelt dug into his chest through his suit jacket, shirt, and tie as the car skidded sideways, tires screaming on the pavement. Random papers, fast-food breakfast wrappers, coins, and other trivial objects flew forward from all parts of the car, including something heavy and hard that he couldn't identify as it struck behind his right ear, pinging his brain like a random text message. His cell phone impacted the windshield and landed face-down on the passenger-side floor. Dave could tell without looking that the phone's face had shattered. Singed rubber burned his nostrils.

Then he saw her. The woman crawled out from the overturned driver's side of the van, her dark hair in disarray and half her shirttail pulled from her jeans. She stood on wobbly legs, staggered forward for thirty feet, and knelt on the pavement.

A solid six, Dave thought. And then he mentally slapped himself. Rating women by their appearance was another character trait he knew he should change.

Dave took his seatbelt off and opened his door almost before he realized he was moving. He ran toward the woman and skidded on his smooth dress shoes like she was home plate and he was trying to beat a strong throw from the outfield.

"Are you okay?" he shouted as he slid beside her, nearly horizontal.

"Jesus!" the woman shouted back, startled by Dave's sudden appearance. Dave saw fear in her dark eyes.

"Back seat," the woman said between coughs as she waved an arm toward the van. "In the back seat!"

Dave rose and ran again, reaching the van with five long strides. He bent to look in the back seat, but the glare made the window opaque. He dropped to his knees and leaned up against the window with his hands alongside his face, making a dark tunnel. The first thing he saw was the shattered window on the other side. Then he saw the upside-down armrests of the back seat. Then he saw a neatly closed umbrella lying on the inverted roof.

And then he saw a child's booster seat, empty and unmoored, overturned near the broken window, the straps dangling free.

He swiveled toward the woman and shouted, "Where's your baby?"

"What?" she called back as she tried to stand.

Dave rose and sprinted toward her. "Your baby!" he screamed. "Where's your ba—"

Before he could finish the word, the toe of his dress shoe caught on a deep crack in the pavement. He found himself suddenly airborne, lurching forward, arms outreached like wings, feeling an instant sense of weightlessness, as if he could glide like that forever. That illusion slipped away as time kept its inevitable pace and gravity tightened its unbreakable grip.

His right knee landed first, and he could feel his fancy slacks ripping, hundreds of dollars' worth of cloth disintegrating as the jagged pavement clawed the fabric. But he could barely feel the skin pulling from his kneecap, more like a caress than an act of violence. Then his left knee slammed into the pavement and, this time, he sensed his skin tearing along with the expensive textile. No gentle caress now, this was an asphalt rasp down to the bone.

His right hand and left elbow hit simultaneously, the thick hide of his palm fusing with the tarred black surface. The delicate skin covering his elbow disappeared as the bone impacted in a fireball of pain. Then his chest, stomach, and hipbones landed in succession, rocking and bouncing in slow motion like a water balloon that somehow wouldn't burst. His face hit last, pulling only thin layers of flesh from his nose, chin, and forehead. But his right cheek, always his best side for selfies, tore away to the molars.

When his dive finally ended, Dave rolled onto his back, the morning sky going in and out of focus high above him. Did the scattered dark clouds foreshadow rain? Or was seeping blood clouding his vision?

The woman lurched into his view and towered above him. He could make out something new in her expression. Fear, yes, but also something adjacent to fear that he couldn't quite identify. She would only look at him for a few seconds, searching instead for points just to his left and then right then near her feet—places to focus away from the unwelcome alterations to his face.

"Baby?" Dave croaked out the word.

She bent down but still couldn't look for long. "What?"

"Your baby," Dave replied. "In the car. Where's your baby?"

"I don't have a baby," she said.

"But the seat?" Dave asked. "The child seat?"

"That's for my sister," she said, straightening. "Well, for my nephew, my sister's baby. An early Christmas present."

She moved away then, and Dave could turn his head just enough to see her walking, steadily now, to the van. He felt a dangling bit of his own face flesh move in the slight breeze.

The woman bent down next to the car, reached in through the broken back seat window, twisted her arm upward—and pulled out a cell phone. She walked back toward Dave but not quite near him, swiping the phone's surface and bringing it to her intact face.

"Yes, hello," she said, twisting slightly to brush dirt from her right hip with the left hand that didn't hold the phone. "There's been a car accident."

Dave almost said that of course he knew about the accident, he was right there, but then he understood that she wasn't talking to him.

"No," she said into her phone. "I'm okay. But there's a guy here, and he needs …" She glanced toward his prone body. "Well, he needs an ambulance, for sure." Dave thought he saw her brow furrow before he noticed that the sky was definitely darkening now as her voice floated toward him from far away.

"No," she said again. "No, he wasn't in the car. He just showed up. I don't know him. He must have thought … Hell. I don't know exactly what he was doing. Just send the goddamned ambulance!"

She looked at Dave now, direct and unblinking. Dave appreciated the eye contact. It was a small kindness, and he wanted to return the feeling but wasn't sure how.

"Now," the woman said into the phone, her voice still drifting but the urgency unmistakable.

Then she said the last words Dave heard that day. "Hurry. Please."

The Miracle of the Dark Suit

That old suit, a conservative brown, had been good enough. The need to wear one was infrequent; the fifteen-year-old suit—the only one I owned—and the brown ones that preceded it had always sufficed.

But the color was wrong. I needed a dark suit; attending a funeral and giving the eulogy while wearing a brown one would not do.

I did not yet know when the funeral would be. Tomorrow, next week, perhaps in a month? Date uncertain made no difference; I best be ready, at least so far as a suit.

In the local department store, I wandered about until locating the men's section, explained to the salesman I had come for a dark suit and quickly chose one, stood still while the alteration marks were placed, and a few days later hung it in my closet.

I was relieved that was done. I was prepared, with regard to clothes if not otherwise, for the funeral and my delivery of the eulogy.

My folks were elderly, and for my dad, the outlook, both intellectually and physically, was particularly grim. A gradual and progressive deterioration had accelerated. He was losing his mind to dementia and could no longer be left alone. Months earlier, when my mom was out one evening, he thought he saw dead bodies in the living room. He called the police who arrived to find no bodies; only pillows arranged neatly, as usual, on the sofa. The confusion that episode evidenced had since become more and more profound throughout the day.

His physical deterioration had likewise rapidly progressed. He was frail and failing; he needed assistance getting in and out of bed and going about the house, often he sat quietly in one place most of the day, frequently dozing. In December he somehow ended up on the floor and was unable to get up, became incontinent, and was finally admitted to the hospital. Stabilized, with life's end appearing clearly within sight, from the hospital he was to go to a nursing home.

There was an excellent facility half a mile from my folks' home, one with which my mom had long been involved as a fundraiser, committee chair, and board member. It was the logical and desired spot for my dad.

He could not go there. Not right away. The dementia unit, "the fifth floor" as it was called, was full. My dad would have to stay elsewhere until a bed became available. As nobody was ever discharged from the dementia unit that meant he would have to wait until somebody there died.

My dad was transferred from the hospital to a nursing home that could accept him on a general care unit where he would stay until "the fifth floor" had an opening. This facility was unhappily inferior—dull, poorly lit, residents left to sit alone for long periods in the hall, grim-faced attendants doing their jobs with little enthusiasm. The mournful environment made our visits to him even more depressing.

So we waited for somebody to die. Somebody. Anybody. The death, whosever it was, would be no great tragedy, more a release from a dark silent prison of dementia. But how was that person any different than my dad? What a strange and confusing wait it was. Should we have been happy when finally the inevitable happened and a bed became available? My dad was transferred.

My mom visited him daily. I visited often, whenever I came to town from my home in the neighboring state. The care was wonderful, a bright and tidy unit with cheerful and dedicated staff. He seemed content enough where he was, he recognized each of us whenever we visited, he did not ask to go back home.

Then, gradually and hardly noticed at first, a strange thing happened. My dad seemed to be getting better. After a few months, he was able to get up from a chair by himself and walk around a bit. More remarkably he became less confused and could carry on a normal conversation. It was an amazing turn of events in what had been a progressive course over the prior few years.

Was it the continuous care he received, the good food—better than my mom's?—or perhaps, and more likely so, the change in his medicines? Whatever the explanation, he improved to the point that my mom brought him back home, unheard of for a patient from "the fifth floor." He still needed care, he still could not be left alone, but he was back home, back in his own house, back with his wife.

Late that summer, a couple of months after my dad had come home, the nursing home scheduled an awards dinner/fundraiser. My mom was one of the honorees because of her many years of service. She hoped we, my wife and I, would attend. Of course, we would.

The theme of the dinner was "Denim and Diamonds." What did that mean and how does one dress for that? My mom thought I should dress appropriately which to her meant a suit. On matters such as this, with her scheduled to receive an award, my mom's opinion was edict.

Since returning home my dad had been reluctant to go out, anxious as to how he would do. When we asked him if he would go to the dinner he had said "maybe." A week later, I in my new suit and my wife lovely as usual, on the evening of the dinner we arrived at my folks' home. There was my dad, neatly dressed and ready to go, my mom coiffed, attractively dressed, and excited as could be. I expected my dad would last for a while and then want to return home; I planned to bring him back and leave him there with an aide who would stay with him.

Off we all went the half mile to the big affair. The one hundred twenty or so guests were outfitted in jeans and denim skirts and such—except for us. But that was okay. It was a good time. There was a lively country band and barbeque-style food. My mom was so happy receiving her award in front of many prominent people, so happy to have her family there to see it and so happy, I am certain, to have us seen there with her.

As for my dad, he did just fine and stayed the entire time. After the dinner was over the band encouraged folks to do some line dancing and a few people did even as others began to leave.

We got up to return home and were slowly working our way toward the exit when my mom, pleased with everything and enjoying herself, began to dance a bit as we gradually worked our way further.

"Come on, dance with me," my mom said to my dad. He stood still for a moment or two and then handed me his cane and began to "dance" with her. He shuffled his feet a little in time with the music, swayed a bit, moved his arms, and had a big smile on his face as did my mom.

I stood there watching this rather extraordinary scene and thought that here I was, in my new dark suit, purchased with my dad's death and funeral in mind. Yet there my folks were, for a few moments at least, as happy as kids in a picture unimaginable to me when I bought the suit. The irony of it all did not escape me and is why I think of that time as *The Miracle of the Dark Suit.*

Flatlands

The country is too flat,
nothing higher than
a prairie dog's mound.
These are mountain
people from the north.
You can feel and see
the disappointment surging
through each of them,
their dejected stance as they
view the constant flatness of
the land as far as they can see.
Tears slip down the elders' cheeks
as they find no mountains here,
no ragged peaks and valleys
across beautiful gray hard granite
with sparkles of blue-green
when the sun flares on layers of lichen,
a dusty crust when dry
but dangerously slippery when wet.
Nothing but flat, flat land for as far
as you can see.

Her Covered Head

The young Muslim woman leaves for work
at a local bank where she's a clerk.
She walks our neighborhood with dread
of those who loathe the cloth around her head,
which shows her devotion to Allah and spouse,
as does her carefully buttoned up blouse.
She treads very lightly on "Christian" sod,
her covered head a lightning rod
for those whose hearts are full of hate,
seeking a scapegoat to berate.
USA born, she's red, white and blue,
with skin that shines with an olive hue.
She's kind to all who cross her path,
so why do some lash out with wrath,
fighting their own Jesus Jihad,
crueler than in Baghdad or Balad?
I'm sure that the Sunday School Jesus I knew
would frown upon this arrogant few,
who tease and torment this sweet girl,
created by God in God's own world.

Mowing the Lawn During a Solar Eclipse

Not total here, so I wasn't sure exactly when
the moon would take its biggest bite from the sun.
And with high clouds, any lessening of light

might be a false sign. But as I passed beneath
the big maple on the riding mower I saw
on the ground where small patches of light shone

through the leaves and branches countless
crescent moons—partial eclipse? I'd no
protective glasses, so I couldn't check

when I emerged from beneath the tree,
but the signs seemed certain. Later,
when I passed again beneath the big maple

to return the mower to the barn and saw no
crescent shapes on the ground, I was sure
I'd witnessed what I dared not see.

Autumn

> "… a west wind lifted
> the wet leaves from the wet ground."
>   —"Isis Unveiled," Edward Hirsch

It's a powerful wind lifts the wet leaves
from the wet ground, heavy as they are,
waiting to sleep through the end of autumn
and all of winter, when, still wet with

snowmelt and the first spring rains, not even
the strongest wind could lift them, matted
together, wedded to the prospect of rot
and rebirth. But for now, in the low light

of autumn, though glistening with moisture
from a late afternoon squall, copper-colored,
yellow and dull red, they are still light enough
to rise up when a west wind blows through,

though they are sluggish and slow and do not
go far and soon lie back down on the ground.

A Minor Theory of Antiquities

Consider this about ancient Egypt:
that those tiny carved or molded forms
that seem so plentiful in museums
were actually children's toys.
This occurred to me today as I
remembered digging in the flower garden
and finding in the soil a toy soldier
several inches down. Even with the dirt
clinging to its creases, I recognized
the plastic form as a toy I'd had
forty-odd years ago and, though I
couldn't recall losing it, must have lost.
Had it lain there for thousands of years
before being discovered, it would now be
meticulously cleaned, given a catalog number
and placed behind glass—or whatever
they'll use in future museums—with
thousands of similar forms dug up and kept.

Lachrymose

    –Summer, 2020

Every day now begins with tears.
As soon as I am upright,
a tear forms in my left eye
and will keep doing so the rest of the day
no matter how many times I dab it
with my shirtsleeve.

They tell me it's actually "dry eyes," somehow,
as if denying the liquid before their eyes,
that my tears may be of poor quality
and my lacrimal gland is overcompensating.

But these are the same eyes
that see the news each morning,
that read of peaceful protestors
sprayed nightly with federal tear gas,
that watch as leaders turn a blind eye,
that witness the eye of our national storm.

And since I cannot touch my face
the few times I am out and about,
for fear of contamination,
the tears trickle down for all to see,
and no amount of cotton or tissue
can stanch how I feel as with my good eye
I see this vale of tears now in sharp relief.

The Sentinel

The knitted brow gives him away.
While others at the meeting choose their diversions—
doodling, working a crossword, starting a new poem—
he takes voluminous notes on nothing,
combing his colleagues' words for discrepancies,
transgressions, for perceived agendas.

Committee reports? Administrative hoops?
Endless lists of new and old business? All grist
for this miller, picking nits out of the previous minutes,
grinding minutiae into fine powder,
then snorting it to maintain his focus.

As we move into the second hour of tedium
and attention wanders for most to picking up the kids,
or the first glass of wine, he's deep in the bunker now,
squinting into the periscope, wary of motions,
amendments from the floor, shooting down
any attempts to circumvent The Rules.

When nearly all is said and done,
when those who have lives will return to them,
when we're down to announcements
and goodbyes and all can sense the ending,
don't even think about asking if there are questions:
His hand is already up.

The Population of Dreams

The number grows year by year,
the faces fresh as yesterday or today,
smiles as real as newly minted coins.

More often than not, they participate
in the storylines, no matter how
tortured or confusing or intricate.

My language deserts me this morning
as I try to reconcile my role long ago
in feeding whatever they had to accept.

Some nights, they play brief walk-ons,
others, speaking roles, in support of
the lead. After all, the script is mine.

Entrance right: they walk into the room,
eye contact, a pause in the step, smiles
either flood or pinpoint the scene in light.

Center stage, back of the head, curls so
familiar, I could extend my hand to touch,
but do not, wait for her to turn, face me.

Stage left, head down, turns to throw me
the stink-eye, disapprobation even I
could not miss or mistake for greeting.

Or worse, somewhere in the second act,
music fades, sounds of activity here rise,
upturned lips turn down. Cold surrounds.

The day is littered with thoughts of night,
the daily rushes flicker back to who they
were, the population of those dreams.

After the Apocalypse, Day 114

Rachid stopped pedaling his bicycle and looked toward the sky. The sun's halo glowed brilliantly along the roof of a Denver skyscraper on the west side of the street. It was after noon for sure. He stepped off his bike, put down the kick-stand, and removed his backpack. He did his best to estimate the direction where east by northeast might be. Dad would have known the right direction. His jaw tightened in irritation. Then shame and sorrow scrunched his eyes. He resolved not to cry and relaxed his face.

He unrolled his prayer mat and cleared his mind of such thoughts, focusing on his prayers.

He used to hate praying. It felt like some duty that had been thrust upon him by a quirk of cultural identity, and he had resented it. He had always performed the prayers mechanically by rote, practically leaping from his mat when he finished them.

Now it was different. Praying filled him with a profound sense of peace. It cleared his mind and his heart. He felt closer to Allah now.

Even so, he wasn't sure precisely where Mecca was or what time he should be praying. He was pretty confident that Allah would forgive him for that, as he had no way of really knowing. And there were no people left to judge him, Muslim or otherwise, in all of Denver. Maybe America. Maybe even the world.

In that sense, he was finally free.

And yet, Rachid could still imagine what many Muslims might say, particularly from the Middle East. That he wasn't a "real" Muslim. That he was an American impostor. Who the hell were they to judge him, anyway? His relationship with Allah was between him and Allah. And he knew it.

There was no one left to force Rachid to be whoever they wanted him to be. He pondered this for a moment. Who did he want to be? Now that he was free of his father's overbearing nature, the prejudice of Christians and Jews, the stereotypes foisted on him by America, and the constant appraisal of his worth by fellow Muslims, what did he actually want?

Rachid slowly rolled up his prayer mat and strapped it to his backpack. As he climbed onto his bike, he remembered where the Denver Public Library was over by North Lincoln Street. They surely must have Aramaic-English dictionaries, Qu'rans, and books about Islam. He could learn to pray properly, not because anyone said to, but because it was a way of showing Allah that he loved Him. He would become his own imam.

A cool breeze blew through his hair, refreshing him. He gazed upward toward heaven. The sky was a deep blue sapphire, unmarred by a single cloud. It was breathtaking.

After the Apocalypse, Day 347

The Grand Haven lighthouse slowly grew taller and wider, blazing scarlet in the morning sun against the misty western sky behind it. Jackson kept his eyes fixed on it as he strode forward, immersed in the surreality of the moment. The cement pier, still wet from last night's rain, squeaked under his shoes with each step. He watched the red grow and grow until the blue on either side disappeared and he was inches away from its surface. They had just repainted the whole lighthouse two years ago, and it was perfect.

For now, anyway. Nobody was ever going to paint it again. In theory, that was okay. There were no more boats. Nobody was going to need it anymore. Jackson understood that, but he also recognized that the giant steel structure would eventually fall into disrepair, the paint would flake away, the metal underneath would rust, and the whole tower would crumble. That would be centuries from now, long after he was gone. Even so, Jackson felt a wistful nostalgia as if he were in that farflung future, wishing back for today.

"Sure, Jackson. That's what you've got to feel melancholy about," he muttered softly, and then he chuckled at the absurdity of such a notion.

He strolled the rest of the way to the end of the pier. Sometimes he still hoped to see old Hank or Marnie sitting in a chair with a fishing pole, like in the old days. A lot of people used to come here to fish. Jackson had never understood how they could have the patience to just sit there all day long.

A seagull caught the breeze coming off of Lake Michigan and let it buoy him upward, and then, spotting something from the corner of his eye, curved a wing and arced downward into the spray. It emerged, joyous and triumphant. There was something majestic and soothing about that. Jackson gazed at the gulls diving for fish for what seemed like hours.

When he finally turned to head back up the pier, he resolved to come back tomorrow morning. Not to look for Hank and Marnie. To watch the gulls. Hell, he might even go into town and find a fishing pole.

After the Apocalypse, Day 421

Tomeika carried her folded stool and plastic bucket out to the row of tomato plants behind her house. She sat down and gingerly pinched the mites and aphids from the leaves of her plants. Many of the tomatoes were starting to color now, but hundreds of little yellow flowers were still forming. This was a good year for tomatoes.

As she shifted her weight, she felt the cell phone in her left pocket press uncomfortably into her hip. She stood up, pulled the phone out of her pocket, and stared at it. The damn thing hadn't been charged in over a year. And it had been even longer since anyone had called her. It was silly to still be carrying it around. She pulled her arm way back, ready to hurl it over the fence into her long-dead neighbor's yard.

No, that wouldn't be right, she reflected. It was funny, how the little things still mattered somehow. The ideas of propriety, respect, civic duty, right and wrong. She walked into the house.

She couldn't put the phone in the trash. There was no one to pick up the trash any more. All of her food waste went into the compost pile in the corner of her property. What to do with an old piece of plastic that nobody needed anymore? She opened a kitchen drawer and slipped it inside.

Bella padded into the room, rubbed against her legs, and purred.

Tomeika picked her up and petted her, looking outside at her dwarf lemon trees. It would still be weeks, maybe longer, before the fruit were ready to be harvested. That was a shame. She yearned for a good lemon. She positively ached for one.

"That's okay Bella. The good things are worth waiting for, right?"

She carried the cat outside and set her down. As Bella prowled the garden for chipmunks, Tomeika walked over to her row of tomato plants. She plucked a ripe plump cherry, popped it in her mouth, and squeezed it between her teeth, feeling the sweet juice across her tongue. She held it in her mouth for almost a minute, savoring the flavor for as long as possible, until she finally had to swallow it.

Humming softly, she resumed tending to her tomatoes.

I Crossed the Water

I crossed the water
in a boat made of glass.

Glass bow, glass stern,
glass wheel,
glass bottom.

The seagulls delighted
in aiming for it.

I could see the fish swimming below,
the plantlife swaying,
the rocks and sand beneath.

And that would sometimes
be beautiful.

But they could see me
just as well.
And they did.

Looking up
with eyes void
and limp.

And I knew the eyes
were there,
but not what
was behind them,

if anything.

And that is what made
crossing the water
unbearable.

The Mayor of New York

Standing in the middle of East 221st Street facing west, I can hear the elevated train. Its rattle and clack brought to me on waves of yellow summer heat. I stare toward the sound like I'm waiting for it to deliver a message. And, there is a message. It's my grandmother, telling me, in her broken English, to get on the sidewalk where I'll be safe: "Ona the side-a-walk where you safe. Watch-a the car."

I hesitate, still trying to grasp the message from the train noise reverberating through Bronx canyons. But behind Granma, Uncle Pete. Pete DeFlorio, former Genovese caporegime, on his way to his retirement job as a bodyguard for entertainers at the Copacabana. He makes a signal, just a flick of his right hand, because Pete DeFlorio rarely needs the spoken word. A gesture will do. And I'm on the sidewalk.

"Get in the car," says he. "I'll take you home."

The Chevy coup, black like most cars of the 1940s, rattles over broken Bronx streets that look like coal in a sea of molten tar.

"Where's your hat," says Uncle Pete. "You don't have anything to cover your head."

"I don't like hats."

"Here! Wear my cap." He puts his Yankees cap on my head with his right hand.

"We have to make a stop first. It's on the way." That is on the way to my home with my parents on Hughes Avenue in Belmont, a Bronx section closer to Manhattan, where my mother and father work, hairdresser and butcher, while my grandparents care for me during vacation.

"I have a job for you," says Uncle Pete. "You have to go to a house and give the box of cookies in the back seat to a man and give him a message. Can you do this?"

"OK," say I. Although the thought of the task makes me nervous.

"Good. His name is Chick Chickoleno. You call him Mr. Chickoleno. Got it? Mr. Chickoleno."

We go through a neighborhood I would later know as Fordham Heights to a brick row house, like my grandparents', but nicer.

"OK. Here's what you do: You go to the door, ring the bell and ask for Mr. Chickoleno. If his wife comes, say you want to see Mr. Chickoleno. He'll be home because it's dinner time. Got me so far?" "Yeah."

"Good. Now, you give the box of cookies to Chick, I mean Mr. Chickoleno! And give him this message: 'Is everything OK with Pete?' When you get the answer, come back to the car; I'll be down the street."

After making me repeat the instructions, Uncle Pete sends me off to meet Mr. Chickoleno, with Italian cookies in a delicate cardboard box fastened with even more delicate string.

The buzzer is, indeed, answered by Mrs. Chickoleno. She's a portly, middle-aged woman with a friendly bearing.

"I want to see Mr. Chickoleno."

"You do, do you. Anybody ever teach you to say please?"

"Please."

"Chick! Chick!" she screams. "There's a little Yankees fan here, wants to talk to you."

Mr. Chickoleno comes to the door, napkin in hand.

He's huge, and I don't feel he has the same friendly bearing as Mrs. Chickoleno, but not scary either. Except that I can see the impression of the handle of a pistol under his underwear shirt, which he wears out.

"Who's this kid? Kid, who are you?"

"Look what he's got in his hands. That will tell you," says Mrs. Chickoleno, pointing to the box of cookies with one hand and holding the other to her forehead like she's about to swoon.

"You with Pete?" says Mr. Chickoleno, taking the box, which he hands off to his wife, who puts it on a slender table holding a lamp, with fringes on the shade, in the form of a beautiful Chinese woman with fringes on her gown's sleeves. I would later come to learn that the lamp's style was known, by some, as "guinea nouveau."

"You with Pete?" Mr. Chickoleno says again, turning back to me.

"Yeah," says I, and stammer: "Is everything OK with Pete?"

"Chick! Fa chrissake, see what the life does to people! A caporegime, and he sends a boy to check things out for him. ... I keep telling you, you have to get out of the life before you end up like this! The paranoia!"

"There is no out!" shouts Mr. Chickoleno. "You're in it for good! I took an oath!"

He holds the napkin up with his right hand like it's a battle flag and with his left signals Mrs. Chickoleno to quiet down. His expression projects a noble purpose.

Then, gently and bending toward me: "Are you related to Pete?"

"He's my uncle."

"Where is he?"

I point down the street.

Mrs. Chickoleno: "Oh, my God! How pathetic!" looking down the street, although I doubt she can spot the car. "You give this message to your uncle," says Mr. Chickoleno with an earnest tone, "that everything is OK, and that he shouldn't worry. OK? And, oh, thanks for the cookies!"

"OK."

"Chick, give the kid something. How old are you little boy?"

"I'm 10."

"Last time Pete sent a girl, his niece, with the cookies. She was older, " says Mrs. Chickoleno.

Mr. Chickoleno takes a roll out of his pocket, big enough to choke a horse. He peels off a 10 and hands it to me as Mrs. Chickoleno smiles approvingly.

"Kid, what are you going to buy with the ten spot?" says Mr. Chickoleno.

I hesitate, then: "A Spalding Hi Bounce ball. ... Maybe a lot of them!"

"He's a Bronx kid! See the hat! A Yankees fan!" says Mr. Chickoleno. "Stick ball! Punch ball! Box ball! They all need a Hi Bounce! "

"I don't know," says Mrs. Chickoleno. "Maybe he should use some of it to light a votary candle and say a prayer to a saint for his uncle."

"Say a prayer to a saint? ... He's a kid. Why would he do that?"

"Well, little boy, I bet you go to a nice Catholic school," Mrs. Chickoleno counters.

"Do you?" adds her husband.

"No."

"Then where? ... It's like pulling teeth with this kid," says she.

"P.S. 21."

"Where's that?"

"Belmont."

"Belmont! How wonderful! You at least take religious instruction at that beautiful Our Lady of Mount Carmel church? ... You know. The Catholic Ca-thechism."

"Yeah, well kinda," I lie. Then, out of annoyance over the interrogation: "No. No, I don't take religious instruction. I don't know the Cathechism."

Mrs. Chickoleno gasps, then looks at me with disgust.

"OK. Enough is enough!" says Mr. Chickoleno. "Lay off the kid! ... What's your name?"

Mrs. Chickoleno: "It doesn't matter." And she slams the door in my face.

Back in the car, Uncle Pete asks how did it go, and is relieved by my response.

"Did he give you any money?" says Uncle Pete.

I show him the 10.

"You did good! Your cousin got only a five," he says with a laugh that sounds more like a cough.

"You keep that money, but give me my hat," which he takes from my head.

He asks what I plan to do with the money, and I give the same answer I gave to the Chickolenos: A Hi Bounce.

Maybe many Hi Bounces, I'm thinking, like the ones I see in their pink glory on the back shelf of Mr. Katz's drugstore, in a wire basket and covered with talc to keep them from sticking together.

"I'll buy you a Hi Bounce," says Uncle Pete. "And, now listen I've got a message for you. I'm going to tell your parents to use the 10 to start a savings account in your name. Then, when you get older, you use the money to go to Fordham University.”

“I’m going to Fordham? Why?”

“So you don’t end up like me!” he shouts with an air of resolve.

And then, with a big smile, says, “And maybe so you can become the mayor of New York!”

An Addictive Personality's Trip to the Tri-State Fair

I'm not really supposed to be here.

For starters, eight overpriced clear
plastic cups of stale
domestic beer melt away
inhibitions—shame has
no place in what's to come.

Carnival games, their flashing
lights hypnotize me into a
necessity for a beta fish.
I shell out dollar after dollar,
crescendoing cursing follows
each time my tossed ping pong ball
ricochets off the narrow openings
of plexiglass fish bowls.
Finally, the vested worker hands
me a thin sandwich-bag
of water with the most
lethargic, pathetic pet fish I've
ever seen. It's fine, I'll
accidentally puncture the bag and
have to trash it later anyway.

Hunger hits and I head
to the midway. Two turkey
legs serve as an appetizer.
No seven-course meal is complete
without the deep-fried main smorgasbord—
traditional footlong corndogs, three
different cheeses-on-sticks,
before proceeding to the avant-
garde culinary experimentation
that is battered butter, bubblegum,
and beer. A bag of cotton candy as a
palate cleanser before I finish with
a few fried oreos and twinkies.

The roaring rides, spinning and dropping,
siren-call to me, the fat fishkiller.
The tilt-a-whirl's centrifugal
effects thrill me. I ride
repeatedly, pausing between only
to shove my head into the
overflowing, acrid aluminium
trash can, right outside the restrooms.

The lights begin to dim
and the cacophony
dimuendos as the crown thins—
a "last call" that, as always, I
ignore.

I am graciously escorted by
a pair of pissed-off security
guards flanking me, their elbows
linked with mine, aiding me
to the front gate.

Next morning, a hangover
permeates my body.

By noon, I'm back on the midway.

Dare Not Blink

     –for the Great Smoky Mountain National Park

Come away from whatever home
to this temperate mountainous zone,
and settle into the dampness,

the ever-present restless sound
of waterfalls and calls of birds.
Keep your eyes open wide

for just one of the Smoky's fifteen
hundred Black bears, just one
Pileated woodpecker, one

Fire Pink. Dare not blink.
You'll miss a common mudpuppy,
a misty vista of depth and color.

Never mind the rain,
wind, insects. In time,
you'll grow to respect each aspect

of this place so full of grace—
this temperate zone's warm tones
of tree trunks, skeletons of Frazier firs

sheltering saplings surviving, believed
resistant to the invasive parasite.
You'll be observed by every animal,

insect, fish and bird. And you'll
come to wonder what you've done
(who you are) to deserve to be so

taken in by your nonhuman kin.

Twelve Rural

There is always an enormous temptation in all of life to diddle around making itsy-bitsy friends and meals and journeys for itsy-bitsy years on end. … We are making hay when we should be making whoopee; we are raising tomatoes when we should be raising Cain, or Lazarus. —Annie Dillard, *Pilgrim at Tinker Creek*

1. According to Cherokee legend, in the beginning there was no land—only sea—and all animals lived in a rock vault in the sky. Water Beetle decided to explore the sea, and dove to the bottom, bringing back soft mud that spread out and became the island called Earth. The flapping of a vulture's wings created mountains, and the animals ordered the sun to move from East to West. Then Kanati (First Man) and Selu (First Woman) were created. This is how it started.

2. There's the barn, but the rules keep changing. Cattle, sheep, goats. Big bales, small bales, fresh green grass. Chickens that lay green eggs and geese that let their young drown in a blue wading pool. Hardheaded rams and softly bleating lambs. You can't get this off TV. You can't make this up to suit the city imagination aching for rural. This isn't the world. This is reality. This is what we have to live with. This is how we see.

3. My gentleman farmer is a mental man, preferring the life of the mind to body work. To climb upon our Deutz tractor these days means scaling Mount Everest, and to gas up the John Deere 4010 is to run a 10K marathon. But talk about Laplace transforms, wave propagation, or vectors, and he's your man. A tractor he can fix, but an idea he can bring to full fruition, graying hair and slower gait notwithstanding.

4. A five-foot-long bull snake hung from the roosting bar in the duck house, its tail section wound tightly around the wooden rod. I grabbed a long stick and coaxed it out, scooted it on its way. It only wanted the duck eggs in the nest, and a higher platform to view from.

5. We feel closed in when the wind struggles hard and the snow grows deep, like beasts that perish at the knife end of hunger, like blurry wires strung across an empty sky, or the darkest parts of judgment. We feel closed in when just outside the door the expanse runs boundless.

6. She was old when we first met her ringing up groceries at a downtown shop. After that, we'd see her push-mowing her own lawn, taking her dog for walks, and sitting at a table while watching a small television in her front room. She sat there alone, watching tv, and anyone driving by could see her and her small

house dilapidated and in critical need of paint. So we got a group together and painted it. She offered us money which we refused. She bought us pizza. No ulterior motive, just one of those random acts of kindness, we assured her. Recently, we heard she fell, broke something, then a short while later, died. The lesson was there: we too often forget about the death and dying part, move through our days thinking we're eternal beings experiencing moments in time. While we're not looking, we reach a decade point, then another. Those younger than us diminish our unbecoming. They're looking in a mirror and they don't like what they see, but we were the same, remember?

7. Three larger people can fit in the cab of this pickup truck. Or four narrow people, maybe five. Like our farm fields and waistlines, our trucks tend to be expansive.

8. Today, peace rises along these just-harvested rows of corn and soybeans. Crops have been torn asunder, passed through heedless war machines, and the land rests. Today, nitrogen has been shot to ground, the ammo limitless, wounds mercilessly inflicted across millions of thunderous acres. There is no Aleppo here, no Boko Haram or Isis. No Saudi Arabia sponsored Lashkar-e-Toba seeking to cause further suffering in Mumbai or Varanasi, no Al-Shabaab about to invade Iowa State University and kill its students. Today, there is no Midwestern war at all, only a quiet surrender of the earth to her keepers.

9. Lock me up for my murderous ways: I routinely kill our front lawn grass by driving onto it in winter to off-load groceries rather than trudging up a snowy slick hill with arms loaded down.

10. We're the product of our roots. I imagine my mother shaking her head as I shake mine. I hear her blunt yet thoughtful analyses as I analyze my own questions and conditions. Her German stalwartness, her raised chin and steadfast eyes, I see them, I am them. This makes for fascinating dialog and friend-keeping in a Facebook world, in a Twitter universe, both too often run afoul of who we are outside a few quick words or a 2D photo trying to approximate a multidimensional existence.

11. Mites from a dying chicken, scabies from the gloves of a handyman, and fleas from a stray kitten. There's power in the secrets we keep, and we each have our own wars to fight.

12. Rural is what we know and what we've become. How hard it is for Iowans to believe in (let alone pay for), say, Tui Na. It's foreign. We'd much rather eat genetically modified produce and feedlot beef, unnatural but at least recognizable. Belief is a system of repeated comforts. The trouble with a one-track mind? There's no middle ground. No room for awe.

Thought I Was Awake

last night a piece of ceiling
fell and no one knew

it did not say a word, just
lay there on the floor looking
up at where it came from

wondering

last night a tree probably fell
in the forest and everyone
    heard it scream
though they wouldn't admit it

thought they were dreaming
but the tree knew better, lying
there on the broken ground

last night I found myself
on the floor without a blanket
or a pillow or a reason

thought I was awake but
    maybe not

thought I saw people
on the wall like flies
compound eyes, round
furry bodies, staring at me

waiting for the blood to dry

tried this morning to pick up
the plaster, put it back where
it came from and fall

into sleep that will not be
broken, into dreams that
will never be the same

Once Again

Once again and once again
if only once again your eyes
could open, eyes could see—
mothers, fathers, daughters,
sons, someone's children
once again

Again and once again
do you need the darkness,
hardened hearts, helpless
shrugs, no light to shine, no
light to shine once again?

Once again and once again
they are children, they are
ours, they are yours, they are
someone's children once again

Again and once again:
George Floyd, Breonna
Taylor, Tamir Rice, Trayvon
Martin, Michael Brown,
Raychard Brooks, Ahmaud
Arbery, more and more
and more once again

blind to faces, blind to tears
you turn your back to them,
but now they will not run away
again, once again and again

Now it's you who feel the need
to run, hide, to give a helpless
shrug, thoughts and prayers
you say, pretended sympathy
with eyes that do not see
that do not want to see

and with open hands, open
wide to money over lives
power over heart, you run away
once again and again, again and

Never again, the children say
Never again once again

Harvesting Bats in the Living Room

they leave you very little choice
as they flutter down the chimney
no Santa with his bag of gifts
they crash in sooty madness
at the ceiling's white agreement
    with the wall

you can only bring them to the floor
with a stinging swing of a tennis racket
or slightly gentler swoop and hiss
    of a nearby butterfly net

you can only weave a wet web
a checkered flag of soggy towels
frayed and heavy over leather wings
    and feathered ears

you can only quell the swelling fear
of bloodlust and rabid death by breathing
deep in rhythm with metallic chirps
    and frantic flapping

as you bring the prehistoric creature
to the waiting door, swing the towel
above you and fling it headlong
    into palpitating darkness

Dee Allen is an African-Italian performance poet based in Oakland, California. Active on the creative writing & Spoken Word tips since the early 1990s. Author of five books (*Boneyard, Unwritten Law, Stormwater,* and *Skeletal Black,* all from POOR Press, and his fifth from Conviction 2 Change Publishing, *Elohi Unitsi*) and 30 anthology appearances (including *Your Golden Sun Still Shines, Rise, Extreme, The Land Lives Forever, Civil Liberties United, Trees In A Garden Of Ashes, Colossus: Home, Impact!* and from Portland, Maine-based Underground Writers Association, *Essential*) under his figurative belt so far.

Glen Armstrong holds an MFA in English from the University of Massachusetts, Amherst and teaches writing at Oakland University in Rochester, Michigan. He edits a poetry journal called *Cruel Garters* and has three current books of poems: *Invisible Histories, The New Vaudeville,* and *Midsummer.* His work has appeared in *Poetry Northwest, Conduit,* and *Cream City Review.*

Cathy Barber's work has been published in many journals, including *SLAB, Sweet, Slant* and *Kestrel,* and anthologies, including *Fire and Rain: Ecopoetry of California.*

Kara Barsalou graduated from Asnuntuck Community College in the Spring of 2020. She has always loved creating and expressing herself on paper, whether it be in a drawing, a painting, or in writing. She has been doing all three of these things religiously since middle school. This is her first published work, and she hopes it can resonate with at least one person!

Paul Beckman is a Connecticut writer whose latest flash collection, *Kiss Kiss* (Truth Serum Press) was a finalist for the 2019/2020 Indie Book Awards. Some of his stories have appeared in *Spelk, Anti-Heroin Chic, Necessary Fiction, Bending Genres, Fictive Dream, Pank, Playboy, WINK,* and *The Lost Balloon.* He had a story selected for the *2020 National Flash Fiction Day Anthology* and was short-listed in the Strands International Flash Fiction Competition. Paul curates the monthly KGB FBomb NY flash fiction reading series (currently virtual).

Robert Beveridge (he/him) makes noise (xterminal.bandcamp.com) and writes poetry in Akron, Ohio. Recent/upcoming appearances in *Blood and Thunder, Feral,* and *Grand Little Things,* among others.

Callie S. Blackstone is a lifelong New Englander. She is lucky enough to wake up to the smell of saltwater and the call of seagulls. Her creative nonfiction has been published in special interest magazine *SageWoman.* It is also forthcoming in *The Manifest-Station.* Her poetry has been published in *The Elephant Ladder.* It is also forthcoming in an anthology titled *Tell Me More* that is being published by East Jasmine Review.

Ace Boggess is author of five books of poetry, including *Misadventure, Ultra Deep Field,* and *The Prisoners.* His writing has appeared in *Harvard Review, Notre Dame Review, Mid-American Review,* and other journals. He received a fellowship from the West

Virginia Commission on the Arts and spent five years in a West Virginia prison. He lives in Charleston, West Virginia.

Gaylord Brewer is a professor at Middle Tennessee State University, where he founded and for 20+ years edited the journal *Poems & Plays*. His most recent books are the cookbook-memoir *The Poet's Guide to Food, Drink, & Desire* (Stephen F. Austin, 2015) and two collections of poetry, *The Feral Condition* (Negative Capability, 2018) and *Worship the Pig* (Red Hen, June 2020).

Melanie Brooks is the author of *Writing Hard Stories: Celebrated Memoirists Who Shaped Art from Trauma* (Beacon Press, 2017). She teaches professional writing at Northeastern University and narrative medicine in the MFA program at Bay Path University in Massachusetts, and creative writing at Nashua Community College in New Hampshire. Her work has appeared in numerous publications, including *Psychology Today, The Washington Post, Ms. Magazine, Creative Nonfiction, The Huffington Post, Modern Loss,* and *Solstice Literary Magazine.* She is completing a memoir called *A Hard Silence* about the lasting impact of living with the ten-year secret of her father's HIV disease before his death in 1995. She lives in New Hampshire with her husband, two children, and two Labs.

Katley Denetria Brown is the pen name for Carol Marrone, who was born in New York City. She grew up in a housing project in the South Bronx and has lived in a number of places, including Minot, North Dakota; Kastellaun, Germany; and Springfield, Massachusetts. Unfortunately, the pandemic has limited her travel options. She gets outdoors as much as possible and looks forward to resuming "normal life" sometime int he future.

Lorraine Caputo is a documentary poet, translator and travel writer. Her works appear in over 180 journals in Canada, the US, Latin America, Europe, Asia, Australia and Africa; and 14 chapbooks of poetry—including *Caribbean Nights* (Red Bird Chapbooks, 2014), *Notes from the Patagonia* (dancing girl press, 2017) and *On Galápagos Shores* (dancing girl press, 2019). In March 2011, the Parliamentary Poet Laureate of Canada chose her verse as poem of the month. Caputo has done over 200 literary readings, from Alaska to the Patagonia. She travels through Latin America, listening to the voices of the pueblos and Earth. Follow her travels at: www.facebook.com/lorrainecaputo.wanderer.

Peter Neil Carroll is currently Poetry Moderator of Portside.org. His latest collection of poetry, *Something is Bound to Break,* (Main Street Rage Press) appeared last year. Earlier titles include *Fracking Dakota;* and *A Child Turns Back to Wave* which won the Prize Americana. His poems have appeared in many print and online journals. He is also the author of a memoir, *Keeping Time* (Georgia).

Joe Cottonwood has repaired hundreds of houses to support his writing habit in the Santa Cruz Mountains of California. His latest book of poetry is *Random Saints.*

Jamie Crepeau is an enthusiastic writer with an active imagination and a strong work ethic. He has had poems published in several literary magazines including *Freshwater, Fresh Ink, Crab Creek Review,* and *Gyroscope Review.* He has a diverse educational background that includes a Bachelor's Degree in Architecture, a Certificate in Manufacturing Technology, and classes in drawing, poetry, 3D printing, and robotics. Working for ten years as an aerospace machinist has taught him to be careful and precise in everything he does, from writing a poem to grinding a gear. Most recently, he has been filming *Magic: The Gathering* videos with his friend Hilary. Please look up theconfusingwords (all one word, no spaces or hyphens) on YouTube to see their work.

Mason Croft was born in Vancouver, Canada. He holds a degree in Theatre from the University of British Columbia. His fiction and food writing has appeared in several journals and anthologies. He currently lives in Singapore.

Shannon Cuthbert is a writer and artist living in Brooklyn. Her poems have appeared in *Bluepper, Collidescope,* and *Chronogram,* among others. Her work is forthcoming in *Ligeia Magazine, Green Silk Journal, The Oddville Press,* and *Schuylkill Valley Journal.*

Susanne Davis is the author of *The Appointed Hour,* a short story collection recently released from University of Wisconsin's Cornerstone Press, and Assistant Professor of Creative Writing at Hope College. She holds an MFA from the Iowa Writers' Workshop. Individual short stories have been published in *American Short Fiction, Notre Dame Review, descant, St. Petersburg Review, Zone 3, Carve,* and numerous others and have won awards and recognition.

Holly Day (hollylday.blogspot.com) has been a writing instructor at the Loft Literary Center in Minneapolis since 2000. Her poetry has recently appeared in *Asimov's Science Fiction, Grain,* and *Harvard Review,* and her newest full-length poetry collections are *Into the Cracks* (Golden Antelope Press), *Cross Referencing a Book of Summer* (Silver Bow Publishing), *The Tooth is the Largest Organ in the Human Body* (Anaphora Literary Press), and *Book of Beasts* (Weasel Press).

Macy Delasco is a Connecticut student with a lifelong love of reading and writing. She lives in a small house with her abnormally large cat, two lizards, and closest confidant. Macy has no idea what she wants to do with the rest of her life, but, regardless, she'll be writing stories throughout.

Steve Denehan lives in Kildare, Ireland, with his wife Eimear and daughter Robin. He is the author of two chapbooks and two poetry collections. Twice winner of Irish Times' New Irish Writing, his numerous publication credits include *Poetry Ireland Review, Acumen, Prairie Fire, Westerly* and *Into the Void.* He has been nominated for Best of the Net, Best New Poet, and The Pushcart Prize.

Josef Desade is an independent author from Manchester, CT. Taking inspiration from the likes of William Blake, Patti Smith, Clive Barker, and more. He has multiple poetry, and fiction books under his belt; as well as features from magazines in the United States and UK. He has created a grassroots following from the ground up. He is currently set to publish the first book in a trilogy in 2021.

Timothy Dodd is from Mink Shoals, West Virginia, and is the author of *Fissures, and Other Stories* (Bottom Dog Press, 2019). His poetry has appeared in *The Literary Review,*

Modern Poetry Quarterly Review, Roanoke Review, Broad River Review, and elsewhere. Also a visual artist, Tim's most recent solo exhibition, "Come Here, Nervousness," was held at Art Underground in Manila, Philippines. His oil paintings can be sampled on his Instagram page, @timothybdoddartwork, and his writing followed on his "Timothy Dodd, Writer" Facebook page. He currently lives and teaches in Philadelphia, PA.

Michael Estabrook has been publishing his poetry in the small press since the 1980s. Hopefully, with each passing decade, the poems have become more clear and concise, succinct and precise, more appealing and "universal." He has published more than twenty collections, a recent one being *The Poet's Curse, A Miscellany* (The Poetry Box, 2019).

Amanda Fahy, age twenty-three, is working towards an English degree at Central Connecticut State University with a minor in writing and publishing. After she graduates graduate, she plans to go on to graduate school and continue her educational career in English. Some of her favorite things include hiking, traveling, and reading.

Nikki Friedman is a social worker by day, and a poet by whenever she has time. She has been writing poetry since she was eight years old, and her first poem was a poem about an abandoned woman during wartime, inspired by an episode of Pokemon. She likes to think that her poetry has gotten better since them. Nikki has a self-published chapbook called *Emotion Words*.

Dave Fromm is the author of a sports memoir entitled *Expatriate Games* (Skyhorse 2008) and a novel entitled *The Duration* (Tyrus/F&W 2016). He lives in western Massachusetts with his wife and kids and is working on a long piece of John Cougar Mellencamp fanfic.

Taylor Graham is a volunteer search-and-rescue dog handler in the California Sierra and served as El Dorado County's inaugural Poet Laureate. In addition to *Freshwater*, her poems appear in *Villanelles* (Everyman's Library), *California Poetry: From the Gold Rush to the Present* (Heyday Books), and *California Fire & Water: A Climate Crisis Anthology*. Her latest collection is *Windows of Time and Place: Poems of El Dorado County* (Cold River Press, 2019).

Dave Gregory is a Canadian writer, a retired sailor, and an associate editor with the Los Angeles-based *Exposition Review*. His work has most recently appeared in *Ellipsis Zine, Write City Magazine*, and *Literally Stories*. Please follow him on Twitter @CourtlandAvenue.

John Grey is an Australian poet, US resident. Recently published in *Soundings East, Dalhousie Review*, and *Connecticut River Review* with work upcoming in *West Trade Review, Willard and Maple* and the *MacGuffin*.

Lee Grossman is a psychoanalyst and photographer who lives and works in Berkeley, California.

Pat Hale's poetry is inspired by both visual art and the natural world. She is the author of the poetry collection, *Seeing Them with My Eyes Closed*, and the chapbook, *Composition and Flight*. Her work appears in many journals, including *CALYX, Sow's Ear, Dogwood, Connecticut River Review*, and *Naugatuck River Review*, and has been awarded CALYX's Lois Cranston Memorial Poetry Prize, and the Sunken Garden Poetry Prize. She lives in Connecticut, where she serves on the board of directors for the Riverwood Poetry Series, Inc., a group which has brought poetry events and festivals to central Connecticut for over twelve years.

Jessica Handly is an author, a college instructor, and the mother of a warrior princess.

Ruth Holzer's poems have appeared previously in *Freshwater Literary Journal* as well as in *Southern Poetry Review, Connecticut River Review, Journal of New Jersey Poets, The South Carolina Review, Blue Unicorn* and *THEMA,* and in other journals and anthologies. A multiple Pushcart Prize nominee, she is the author of five chapbooks, most recently *A Face in the Crowd* (Kelsay Books, 2019) and *Why We're Here* (Presa Press, 2019).

Zebulon Huset is a teacher, writer, and photographer living in San Diego. His writing has recently appeared in *Freshwater Literary Journal, Meridian, The Southern Review, Fence, Rosebud, Atlanta Review & Texas Review,* among others. He publishes the writing prompt blog *Notebooking Daily* and edits the journal *Coastal Shelf.*

James Croal Jackson (he/him/his) is a Filipino-American poet. He has a chapbook, *The Frayed Edge of Memory* (Writing Knights Press, 2017), and recent poems in *Sampsonia Way, San Antonio Review,* and *Jam & Sand.* He edits *The Mantle Poetry* (themantlepoetry.com) and works in film production in Pittsburgh, Pennsylvania. (jamescroaljackson.com)

Andrew Jarvis is the author of *The Strait, Landslide,* and *Blood Moon.* His poems have appeared in *Cottonwood, Measure, Bombay Gin,* and others. He holds high honors from the Nautilus, INDIE Book of the Year, and NextGen Indie Book Awards. Andrew holds an M.A. in Writing from Johns Hopkins University.

Genevieve Jaser is a senior at Southern Connecticut State University. She often writes about the odd and unpredictable nature of human behavior and emotions; she believes the more we recognize our own strangeness, and pick up a pen to dissect it, the more we may be able to find solace for ourselves and others. She believes in the power of art and language—the ability for writing to enlighten, teach, and unite us, and, maybe most importantly, its ability to get us to start looking inward and around in order to question and look closely. She is the current Editor of *Folio,* and her work has been published most recently in *Blue Muse Magazine, Ginosko Literary Journal,* and *Circumference.*

Brandon L. Kroll is a current student at Asnuntuck Community College who is finishing his associate degree in Liberal Arts. He is hoping to transfer to a school in Virginia next year where he intends to finish his bachelor's in fine arts. Brandon has been writing since he was eleven years old and has always had a passion for stories. He hopes to one day write a fantasy trilogy.

John Lambremont Sr., is a poet and writer from Baton Rouge, Louisiana, where he lives with his wife and their little dog. John holds a B.A. in Creative Writing and a J.D. from Louisiana State University. He is the former editor of *Big River Poetry Review*, and has been nominated for The Pushcart Prize. John's poems have been published internationally in many reviews and anthologies, including *Pacific Review, Flint Hills Review, The Minetta Review, Sugar House Review,* and *The Louisiana Review.* John's full-length poetry collections include *Dispelling The Indigo Dream* (Local Gems Poetry Press 2013), *The Moment Of Capture* (Lit Fest Press 2017), *Old Blues, New Blues* (Pski's Porch Publishing 2018), and *The Book Of Acrostics* (Truth Serum Press 2018). His chapbook is *What It Means To Be A Man (And Other Poems Of Life And Death)*, published in 2014 by Finishing Line Press. John enjoys music, playing his guitars, fishing, and old movies. He has battled pancreatic cancer since 2018.

Tom Legasse's poetry has been published in *Faith, Hope & Fiction, Silver Birch Press Prime Movers Series, Freshwater Literary Journal, Word Mill Magazine, The Monterey Poetry Review, Wine Drunk Sidewalk, Plum Tree Tavern, iamnotasilentpoet.com,* and *Wax Poetry & Art,* along with a half dozen anthologies. He lives in Bristol, Connecticut.

Sarah Leslie holds an MFA from California Institute of the Arts. Her fiction was named a semi-finalist for the American Short(er) Fiction Prize and her nonfiction earned Disquiet International Notable Mention. She is a former participant of Bread Loaf in Sicily and of the 2021 Tin House Workshop. Her writing has been published in *Barnstorm Journal, K'in Literary Journal,* and *Tiny Seed Journal,* among others. She writes and farms in the mountains of Liguria, Italy, with her husband and his family.

Christopher Linforth has recently published work in *Epiphany, Notre Dame Review, The Millions,* and other magazines.

DS Maolalai has been nominated seven times for Best of the Net and three times for the Pushcart Prize. His poetry has been released in two collections: *Love is Breaking Plates in the Garden* (Encircle Press, 2016) and *Sad Havoc Among the Birds* (Turas Press, 2019)

Joan McNerney's poetry is found in many literary magazines such as Seven Circle Press, Dinner with the Muse, Poet Warriors, Blueline, and Halcyon Days. Four Bright Hills Press Anthologies, several Poppy Road Review Journals, and numerous Spectrum Publications have accepted her work. She has four Best of the Net nominations. Her latest title is The Muse in Miniature available on Amazon.com and Cyberwit.net

Rosemary Dunn Moeller has had poems published by *Alembic, Aurorean, Vermont Literary Review, Mobius, Patterson Literary Review, Penmen Review* and many other literary journals. She's had two chapbooks published by Four Quarters to a Section SDSPS: *Midnight Picnic in the Fields and The Lift of Wind Across Wings.* She writes to connect to others, has traveled with her husband to all seven continents. They farm half the year on the prairie and spend half the year on the ocean.

Luiz Emanuel de Castro Moura (Manny) is a senior theatre student at Capital Community College. He has worked with West Hartford Community Theater and West

Hartford Summer Arts Festival. Manny believes that art is the best way to express yourself.

John Muro is a life-long resident of Connecticut and a graduate of Trinity College. He has also attained advanced degrees from Wesleyan University and the University of Connecticut. His professional career has focused on environmental stewardship and conservation, and he currently lives in Guilford with his wife, Debra. They have four children. John's first volume of poems, *In the Lilac Hour,* will be published this fall by Antrim House, and his poetry has been praised by Robert Cording, former Connecticut poet laureate Rennie McQuilkin, and others.

Zach Murphy is a Hawaii-born writer with a background in cinema. His stories appear in *Reed Magazine, Ginosko Literary Journal, The Coachella Review, Mystery Tribune, Yellow Medicine Review, Ellipsis Zine, Drunk Monkeys, Wilderness House Literary Review,* and *Flash: The International Short-Short Story Magazine.* His forthcoming chapbook *Tiny Universes* (Selcouth Station Press) is due out in Spring 2021. He lives with his wonderful wife Kelly in St. Paul, Minnesota.

Elise O'Reilly is a graduate of Asnuntuck Community College and the single mother of two boys, ages eleven and five. Her boys are her world, and she has plans to write about her life as a newly single mom in the pandemic. Currently, her poetry focuses on mental health and the hard times she has been through. For Elise, sorting and arranging the words to express her hardships has helped her to process them and move forward.

Victoria Orifice wishes memoir came naturally to them, but it's difficult enough thinking about the past let alone writing it. They much prefer far-off fantasies where the ghosts of the past can't haunt them outside of thinly veiled metaphors. Once wrote a story titled ";" which people seemed to like.

After her retirement from medical practice, **Ruth Pagano** decided to take up creative writing as a hobby. Most of her work has been poetry, several of which have been published, but now she is using more of her personal experiences for memoir writing.

S.E. Page is the co-editor of *Young Ravens Literary Review* and a Pushcart Prize nominee. Her poetry has been published in journals including *Connecticut River Review, Star*Line, Oakwood,* and *NonBinary Review.* Page also writes novels and blogs at iffymagic.com.

Wood Reede has been featured in *(mac)ro(mic), Cobalt Review, Puerto del Sol,* and *Quiet Lightning.* Her YA novel, *Remy,* was a semifinalist for the Allegra Johnson Prize in Novel Writing. She lives in Los Angeles with her husband, son, their opinionated, one-eyed rescue cat, and Watson, their Miniature Schnaupin. www.woodreede.com

Seven-time Pushcart Prize nominee **Russell Rowland** writes from New Hampshire's Lakes Region, where he has judged high-school Poetry Out Loud competitions. His latest poetry book, *Wooden Nutmegs,* is available from Encircle Publications.

Natalie Schriefer often writes about women in sports. She received her MFA from Southern Connecticut State University and works as a freelance writer and editor. Home base: www.natalieschriefer.com.

Edythe Haendel Schwartz is the author of two poetry collections, *A Palette of Leaves,* Mayapple Press, and *Exposure,* Finishing Line Press. Her poems appear widely in journals and anthologies, including *Freshwater Literary Journal, Faultline, Potomac Review, Cave Wall,* and *The Southern Review,* among others.

Emily Schwartz is a Bunnell High School graduate who is currently attending Housatonic Community College. They are striving for a transfer degree in English and aim to be a writer.

John Sheirer (pronounced "shy-er") has taught writing and communications for twenty-eight years at Asnuntuck Community College in Enfield, Connecticut. He writes a monthly column on current events for the *Daily Hampshire Gazette,* and his books include memoir, fiction, poetry, essays, political satire, and photography. His recent book, *Fever Cabin,* is a fictionalized journal of a man isolating himself during the current pandemic. (All proceeds from this book benefit pandemic-related charities.) Find him at JohnSheirer.com.

Harvey Silverman is a retired physician living in New Hampshire who writes nonfiction primarily for his own enjoyment. His nonfiction stories have appeared in *Ocotillo Review, Queen's Quarterly, Hadassah Magazine, Freshwater Literary Journal,* and elsewhere.

Richard Smith has been writing poetry since 1985 and did his first four open-mic readings in Las Vegas in 1987. He has read in many bookstores, coffee shops, libraries, and on Pittsfield Community TV for many years, and has been involved with *Freshwater Literary Journal* since its beginning in 2000. In 2018, U.S. Representative Joe Courtney presented Richard with a Korean Ambassador for Peace Medal and a Bronze Star that he earned while serving in the Navy during the Korean War from August 1947 to March 1952.

Susan Winters Smith was born in Massachusetts, raised in Vermont, and has lived in Connecticut for fifty years. She has been writing all her life, has been a journalist with published poems and genealogy articles. She has self-published seven books, including novels, children's fiction, poetry, and humor.

Matthew J. Spireng's 2019 Sinclair Prize-winning book *Good Work* was published in 2020 by Evening Street Press. A ten-time Pushcart Prize nominee, he is the author of two other full-length poetry books, *What Focus Is* and *Out of Body,* winner of the 2004 Bluestem Poetry Award, and five chapbooks.

Steve Straight's books include *The Almanac* (Curbstone/Northwestern University Press, 2012) and *The Water Carrier* (Curbstone, 2002). He was professor of English and director of the poetry program at Manchester Community College, in Connecticut.

Eugene Stevenson is the son of immigrants, the father of expatriates. His poems have appeared in *Adelaide Literary Magazine, Angel City Review, DASH Literary Journal, Dime Show Review, Gravel Literary Magazine, The Hudson Review, October Hill Magazine, The Poet Magazine, South Florida Poetry Journal, Swamp Ape Review,* and *Tipton Poetry Journal.*

Kelly Talbot has been an editor for Wiley, Macmillan, Oxford, Pearson Education and other major publishers. His writing has appeared in dozens of magazines and anthologies. He divides his time between Indianapolis, Indiana, and Timisoara, Romania.

John Tustin's poetry has appeared in many disparate literary journals in the decade since he began to write again. fritzware.com/johntustinpoetry contains links to his published poetry online.

Charles R. Vermilyea Jr. is a retired *Hartford Courant* copy editor. University of Connecticut graduate (1967), English/history. Army, 2/10 Cavalry Buffalo Soldiers (Korea, 1962-63). Son Jon, a California artist. Daughter Elizabeth, a New York actress. War veteran poet Brian Turner said Vermilyea's writing shows "a strong sense of voice, and that'll carry your stories a long way to catch (and keep) the reader's attention."

Shelby Wilson writes, teaches, and lives in Amarillo, Texas. He holds a B.A. in English from Texas A&M University and an M.A. in English from West Texas A&M University. His writing has appeared in many publications, including *Ink & Nebula, Sparks of Calliope, Backchannels, BeZine,* and anthologies from Madness Muse Press and Elizabeth River Press.

Diana Woodcock is the author of seven chapbooks and three poetry collections, most recently *Tread Softly* (FutureCycle Press, 2018) and *Near the Arctic Circle* (Tiger's Eye Press, 2018). Her two books forthcoming in 2021 are *Facing Aridity* (a finalist for the 2020 Prism Prize for Climate Literature, Homebound Publications) and *Holy Sparks* (Paraclete Press). Recipient of the 2011 Vernice Quebodeaux Pathways Poetry Prize for Women for her debut collection, *Swaying on the Elephant's Shoulders,* her work appears in *Best New Poets 2008* and has been nominated for Best of the Net and the Pushcart Prize. Currently teaching in Qatar at Virginia Commonwealth University's branch campus, she holds a PhD in Creative Writing from Lancaster University, where her research was an inquiry into the role of poetry in the search for an environmental ethic.

Chila Woychik is originally from the beautiful land of Bavaria. She has been published in numerous journals including *Cimarron* and *Passages North,* and has released an essay collection, *Singing the Land: A Rural Chronology* (Shanti Arts, 2020). She won *Storm Cellar*'s 2019 Flash Majeure Contest and *Emry*'s 2016 Linda Julian Creative Nonfiction Award. These days she tends sheep, chickens, and two aging barn cats, and roams the Iowan outback. She also edits the *Eastern Iowa Review.* www.chilawoychik.com

James K. Zimmerman's writing appears in *American Life in Poetry, Chautauqua, Nimrod, Pleiades, Salamander,* and *Vallum,* among others. He is author of *Little Miracles* (Passager, 2015) and *Family Cookout* (Comstock, 2016), winner of the Jessie Bryce Niles Prize.

Notice of Non-discrimination: Asnuntuck Community College does not discriminate on the basis of race, color, religious creed, age, sex, national origin, marital status, ancestry, present or past history of mental disorder, learning disability or physical disability, sexual orientation, gender identity and expression or genetic information in its programs and activities. In addition, the College does not discriminate in employment on the basis of veteran status or criminal record. The following individuals have been designated to handle inquiries regarding the non-discrimination policies: Tim St. James, Interim Dean of Students/Title IX Deputy, tstjames@asnuntuck.edu (860) 253-3011 and Deborah Kosior, 504/ADA Coordinator, AS-Disability Services@asnuntuck.edu (860) 253-3005, Asnuntuck Community College, 170 Elm Street, Enfield, CT 06082.